Reuben Briggs Davenport

The Death-Blow to Spiritualism

Reuben Briggs Davenport

The Death-Blow to Spiritualism

ISBN/EAN: 9783337389154

Printed in Europe, USA, Canada, Australia, Japan

Cover: Foto ©Lupo / pixelio.de

More available books at **www.hansebooks.com**

OCT. 1897.   ISSUED MONTHLY. $6.00 PER YEAR.
ENTERED AT THE NEW YORK POST OFFICE AS SECOND-CLASS MATTER.

THE
DEATH-BLOW
TO
SPIRITUALISM:

BEING

THE TRUE STORY OF THE FOX SISTERS, AS RE-
VEALED BY AUTHORITY OF MARGARET FOX
KANE AND CATHERINE FOX JENCKEN.

BY

REUBEN BRIGGS DAVENPORT.

NEW YORK:
G. W. *Dillingham* Co., *Publishers.*
MDCCCXCVII.

Copyright, 1888.
BY
REUBEN BRIGGS DAVENPORT.

[*All Rights Reserved.*]

GIFT

TO

MRS. HESTER S. DWINELLE.

"ALONSO. This is as strange a maze as ere men trod,
And there is in this business more than nature
Was ever conduct of: some oracle
Must rectify our knowledge.
   "PROSPERO.   Sir, my liege,
Do not infest your mind with beating on
The strangeness of this business : at picked leisure,
Which shall be shortly, single I'll resolve you
(Which to you shall seem probable) of every
These happen'd accidents : till when be cheerful,
And think of each thing well.—Come hither, spirit;
Set Caliban and his companions free:
Untie the spell."

SHAKESPEARE.—*The Tempest.*

PREFACE.

This book has been written in extreme haste. It does not pretend to literary style. But it pretends to absolute truthfulness and a reverent regard for justice.

Its sole value is its character as a contribution to the real history of Spiritualism. As such, it is unquestionably of great importance, greater even than any work of the kind that has been published since the beginning of modern Spiritualism.

It is, in fact, what its title sets forth—"THE DEATH-BLOW TO SPIRITUALISM."

No one who does not love illusion for illusion's sake—better, in other words, than he loves the truth—can, after reading this volume, remain a follower of Spiritualism and its hypocritical apostles.

The full authorization of Mrs. MARGARET FOX KANE and Mrs. CATHERINE FOX JENCKEN for the publication of this work will be found on the next to the following page.

29th October, 1888.

We hereby approve of Mr. Reuben B. Davenport's design to write a true account of the origin of Spiritualism and of our connection therewith, and we authorize him to make proper use of all data and material that we furnish him.

New York, 15th Oct., 1888.

Margaret Fox Kane
Catherine Fox Jencken

CONTENTS

I.

INTRODUCTION.

Poetic Justice of the Exposure. 13

II.

RENUNCIATION.

Chapter.   Page
I. "God Has Not Ordered It." . . . 25
II. The Discomfited Enemy. 39
III. A Second Blow. 53
IV. The Hand of the Persecutor. . . . 60
V. Solemn Abjuration. 65

III.

HISTORY.

VI. Origin of the Fraud. 81
VII. Garbled and Distorted Testimony. . . 94

CONTENTS.

Chapter	Page
VIII. Development of the Fraud.	102
IX. The Mercenary Campaign.	121
X. Spiritualistic Boomerangs.	131
XI. The Supreme Audacity of Fraud.	150
XII. A Scientific Jury.	164
XIII. The Unalterable Verdict.	201

IV.

REPENTANCE.

XIV. The Heart Pleads for the Soul.	209
XV. From Shadow to Light.	231

INDEX. 241

I.
INTRODUCTION.

INTRODUCTION.

POETIC JUSTICE OF THE EXPOSURE.

That the inventors of an infamous fraud should deal to it its death-blow, is the poetic justice of fate.

Over the creature, the creator has power of life and death.

The creators of Spiritualism abjure its infamy.

They decree its death.

They condemn it to final destruction.

They fasten upon those who continue to practice it the obloquy of history, and the scorn of mankind for all time to come.

Margaret and Catharine Fox, the youngest of three sisters, were the first to produce "spiritualistic manifestations."

They are now the most earnest in denunciation of those impostures; the most eager to dissipate the foolish belief of thousands in the flimsiest system of deception that was ever cloaked with the hypocrisy of so-called religion.

When, as by accident, they discovered a method of deceiving those around them by means of mysterious noises, they were but little children, innocent of the thought of wrong, ignorant of the world and the world's guile, and imagining only that what they did was a clever lark, such as the adult age easily pardons to exuberant and sprightly youth.

Not to them did the base suggestion come that this singular, this simple discovery, should be the means of deluding the world, of exalting them in the minds of the weakly credulous and of bringing them fame and splendor and sumptuous pleasure.

No one who learns their true history can still believe them guilty of the willful inception of this most grotesque, most transparent and corrupting of superstitions.

The idea had its monstrous birth in older heads, heads that were seconded by hearts lacking the very essence of truth and the fountain of honest human sympathy.

The two children, who had at first delighted, as younglings will, in what was but a laughable mystification, were dragged into a sordid, wicked and loathsome speculation, built upon lying and fraud, as unforgivable as the sin of Satan, and of which they were but the unthinking instruments, often reluctant and remorseful, yet docile and compliant by nature.

Thus the "Rochester knockings," the example and prototype of all later so-called spiritualistic "phenomena," began merely in a curious childish freak, disguised without effort, and which, from the first, was encouraged to partly formed understandings by the wonder and intense spirit of inquiry it provoked.

The young operators were carried away by the undreamt-of current of enthusiasm and awe in which they soon became involved. They felt the natural need of maintaining with unabating dexterity, that false sense of the miraculous which by chance they had called forth.

Thus they went from one stage to another of this queer illusion, and, being compelled by a harder and more mature intelligence to repeat their part over and over again, became the chief means of establishing that injurious belief in communications from the spirits of the departed, of which such great numbers have become the victims.

Many an older offender against common sense, reason and strict morality persists through force of circumstance in the pathway he has chosen, and does not turn backward, merely because he cannot do so without wearing the face of shame.

From such slight and trivial beginning came the great movement—great because of the number which it comprised and of the sensation which attended its progress—that for more than forty years has alternately surprised, puzzled, disgusted and amused the world.

From so little a plant has grown a gigantic weed of deceit, corruption and fraud, nurtured upon the fattening lust of money, and of the flesh.

What has developed from it is not alone a system of so-called communications through a puerile code of signals with an unseen world; but, as Dante describes, in his incomparable epic, forms of monstrosity which combine a hideous human semblance and a loathly animal foulness, so this venomous evil has become conglomerate in its hateful phases of delusion, and its petty sordidness and depravity.

Thus the Tuscan bard describes the spirit of fraud:

"'Lo! the fell monster with the deadly sting!
Who passes mountains, breaks through fenced walls
And firm embattled spears, and with his filth
Taints all the world! Thus me my guide addressed,
And beckon'd him, that he should come to shore,
Near to the stony causeway's utmost edge.
"Forthwith that image vile of fraud appear'd,

His head and upper part expos'd on land,
But laid not on the shore his bestial train.
His face the semblance of a just man's wore.
So kind and gracious was its outward cheer;
The rest was serpent all; two shaggy claws
Reach'd to the armpits, and the back and breast,
And either side, were painted o'er with nodes
And orbits. Colors variegated more
Nor Turks nor Tartars e'er on cloth of state
With interchangeable embroidery wove,
Nor spread Arachne o'er her curious loom.
As ofttimes a light skiff, moor'd to the shore,
Stands part in water, part upon the land;
Or, as where dwells the greedy German boor,
The beaver settles watching for his prey;
So on the rim, that fenced the sand with rock,
Sat perched the fiend of evil. In the void
Glancing, his tail upturn'd its venomous fork,
With sting like scorpion's armed."

The world has not seen in all its long procession of follies, vagaries, and strange mania, one so utterly devoid of a reasonable foundation as this.

Yet none has been more eagerly believed; and

this very tendency has evolved into so strong a desire to believe that thousands of those who have professed to investigate it have done so only ostensibly, their eyes, figuratively speaking, tightly bandaged, to shut out everything but the artificial vision that they were most eager to see.

It is to be hoped that the world will now form its ultimate conclusion upon this flagrant and audacious system of humbuggery :—that, regarded as a superstition, it ranks even below voudooism and fetich-worship, and, as an illusion, below the effects produced by the most ordinary magician at a country fair.

Dragged into this life when infants, rescued from it for an interval by two men* whose names are historical, the one as a hero and explorer, the other as a journalist and daily philosopher ; borne back to it again by the tide of ill-fortune ; used and controlled, by those whose hearts were "dry as summer's dust," for their own hateful purposes ; menaced when conscience rebelled and

* Dr. Kane and Horace Greeley.

suggested retraction and amends; driven to seek momentary oblivion of their present degradation in a vice that was the result of their enforced public career; finally, persecuted in a stealthy and treacherous way by those who had profited most by the fraud that they had set up, because it was feared that sooner or later they could no longer keep silent and would betray its real origin; seeing their existence slipping away from them with nothing but Dead Sea fruit remaining to their bitter portion; feeling more and more the need of an atonement to conscience and the opinion of the world—-Margaret and Catherine Fox now denounce and anathematize Spiritualism as absolutely and utterly false from beginning to end; and they declare their solemn intention to devote themselves henceforth to the noble task of undoing the great evil which they have done, and of leaving no single stone of foundation behind them for weak-minded future generations to base a futile faith upon.

In these pages will be found the full and

truthful story of Spiritualism, as it was and is, as gathered from the lips of both Margaret Fox Kane and Catharine Fox Jencken, and verified by letters, documents and published data. It is written with their full knowledge and earnest sanction.

The bold fabric of lies built up to sustain the claim that the "rappings" in which all spiritualistic so-called phenomena originated were unaccountable except on the supernatural hypothesis, can no longer be cited to an intelligent mind. The elaborate narrative published by the eldest sister, Mrs. Ann Leah Fox Underhill, who is now the only remaining stay of spiritualistic deception, is proven to be false from title-page to finis.

I have given in the following pages, the real lives of Mrs. Kane and Mrs. Jencken, in so far as they bear in any important degree upon the development of the fraud of Spiritualism.

II.

RENUNCIATION.

CHAPTER I.

GOD HAS NOT ORDERED IT.

The world of "spiritualists" and non-spiritualists was startled on the 24th of September, 1888, by the publication in the New York *Herald*, of an article with the following head-lines:

"GOD HAS NOT ORDERED IT."

A Celebrated Medium Says the Spirits Never Return.

CAPTAIN KANE'S WIDOW.

One of the Fox Sisters Promises an Interesting Exposure of Fraud.

To many, an article of this kind seemed in a degree sensational. Not to those, however, who had previously had some inkling of the secret history of Spiritualism, and who for years had looked for the day of its inevitable confounding.

A sudden disclosure like this, by one of the "Mothers of Spiritualism," if the term may be used, suggested a sort of reckless vagary, a species of extravagance, due, as might have been fancied, to some abnormal condition of the mind.

Yet to those who had had an intimate acquaintance with Maggie Fox Kane this step had long been foreshadowed. As will appear later, no one could have imagined the real intensity of moral pain that for years she had endured.

In recent years, both she and her sister, Catharine Fox Jencken, had been but poorly provided with this world's goods. Obliged to depend almost wholly on themselves for support, they had dropped more and more out of sight, till the public at last hardly recognized their names, if perchance they appeared in print, as those of the principal instruments in the founding of Spiritualism. For this, there was a reason. It was a deep-seated and long increasing disgust with their fraudulent profession—the fuller realization to their minds, as their knowledge of the world grew broader, of the monstrous evil to which, innocently at first, they had given birth. So at intervals they were filled with despairing despondency and remorse. Their weaknesses, their self-indulgence, their lack of providence for themselves, are largely attributable to these causes. It could not be said of them that they were ever remarkably selfish, or cold-hearted or calculating. Such a character, however, has of right been coupled with the name of their elder sister, who by reason of the ties of blood and of her older experience ought long ago to have led them out of the by-ways of imposture, instead of persistently seeking to shut off their escape from this horrible bondage, and to plunge them deeper into the mire of guilt and infamy, so that the chance of their rising above it, and denouncing it, might grow less and less.

The impulse to set herself right on the record of the world, after years of enslavement in the hateful gyves of charlatanism, must stand to Maggie Fox's credit alone. It sprang from her own bosom, not from the inspiration, suggestion or persuasion of any one else. Returning from Europe in September, 1888, after a peculiar experience, which had convinced her that those chiefs of spiritualistic fraud who feared her and her sister, because they held the key of the whole of the artificial mystery, were bent upon persecuting them into an abject silence, she at once put in execution the resolution which had been so long in process of growth, but until then had never been fully ripened.

This was to effect the unqualified exposure of the false system of Spiritualism. She naturally chose as a medium for her repentant message to the world, that great cosmopolitan journal, the *New York Herald*, which is known in every corner of the earth, and is ever ready to perform an important service to mankind. Before she started on her homeward voyage, she committed herself once and for all to this courageous and worthy step.

The disclosures regarding the notorious Madam Diss De Barr had offended Mrs. Kane more than anything which had occurred in Spiritualism in a long time, for they presented the enforced association of her name and the simple, childish origin of the "Rochester knockings," with the gross and revolting frauds which had been their outgrowth. So imbued had she become, by this time, with the idea that the developed system of Spiritualism was something to be loathed, as Milton loathed the hideous creature who sat by the inner portals of hell, that words could not express her utter scorn and hatred of this common woman, who posed as an agent of sacred communications between the living and the dead.

The New York *Herald* of May 27, 1888, contained this letter, written by Mrs. Margaret Fox Kane in London :

THE CURSE OF SPIRITUALISM.

Gower Street, Bedford Square, W. C.,
London, May 14, 1888.

To the Editor of the Herald :

I read in the *Herald* of Saturday, May 5, an account of the sad misfortune that has befallen my dear sister Katie, Mrs. Kate Fox Jencken, and in the article it is stated that I am still a resident of New York, which is a mistake. I sailed for England on the 22d of March, and I presume my absence has added to my darling sister's depressed state of mind. The sad news has nearly killed me. My sister's two beautiful boys referred to are her idols.

Spiritualism is a curse. God has set His seal against it ! I call it a curse, for it is made use of as a covering for heartless persons like the Diss De Barrs, and the vilest miscreants make use of it to cloak their evil doings. Fanatics like Mr. Luther R. Marsh, Mr. John L. O'Sullivan, ex-Minister to Portugal, and hundreds equally as learned, ignore the "rappings" (which is the only part of the phenomena that is worthy of notice) and rush madly after the glaring humbugs that flood New York. But a harmless "message" that is given through the "rappings" is of little account to them ; they want the "spirit" to come to them in full form, to walk before them, talk to them, to embrace them, and all such nonsense, and what is the result? Like old Judge Edmonds and Mr. Seybert, of Philadelphia, they become crazed, and at the direction of their fraud "mediums" they are induced to part with all their worldly possessions as well as their common sense, which God intended they should hold sacred. Mr. Marsh's experience is but another example of hundreds who have preceded him.

No matter in what form Spiritualism may be presented, it is, has been and always will be a curse and a snare to all who meddle with it. No right minded man or woman can think otherwise.

I have found that fanatics are as plentiful among "inferior men and women" as they are among the more learned. They are all alike. They cannot hold their fanaticism in check, and it increases as their years increase. All they will ever achieve for their foolish fanaticism will be loss of money, softening of the brain and a lingering death.

MARGARET F. KANE.

This anathema dismayed those who had basely profited by Spiritualism, and it brought a deeper shock to the hearts of many who were sincere believers. The publication, however, in the

Herald, three months later, of an interview with Mrs. Kane on her arrival in this city, the striking head-lines of which I have cited above, capped the climax of consternation. This article is well worthy of reproduction.

The eccentric circles wherein "isms" reign in discordant supremacy will be probably as deeply exercised over an approaching exposure of the tricks and illusions of Spiritualism, as they were over the rude logic of common sense and justice which drew aside the thin veil of fraud in the case of Madam Diss De Barr, and revealed the real nature of her flimsy system of deception in all its vulgar absurdity.

I called yesterday at a modest little house in West Forty-fourth street, and was received by a small, magnetic woman of middle age, whose face bears the traces of much sorrow and of a world-wide experience. She was negligently dressed, and she was not in the calmest possible mood. But she knew what she was talking about when, in response to my questions, she told a story of as strange and fantastic a life as has ever been recorded, and declared over and over again her intention of balancing the account which the world of humbug-loving mortals held against her, by making a clean breast of all her former miracles and wonders. In intervals of her talk, when she had risen from her chair, and paced the room, or had covered her face with her hands and almost sobbed with emotion, she would seat herself suddenly at a piano and pour forth fitful floods of wild, incoherent melody, which coincided strangely with that reminiscent weirdness which, despite its cynical reality, still characterized the scene.

This woman, albeit a notorious career has classed her with mountebanks and worse in the minds of reasonable beings, had yet by some element or other in her character retained a degree of public respect. Perhaps it is because months ago she abandoned the art of deception and has since to her intimate friends evinced no ordinary measure of contempt for all who still pursue it. She is known on both sides of the Atlantic, and when in London, is entertained by some of the best-to-do of the great and comprehensive middle class.

Circumstances had brought me to this house, and I did not at first know her. I soon found, however, that this was the most famous of the celebrated trio of witches, the Fox sisters, among the earliest spiritualistic mediums in this country. She is also the widow of Dr. Elisha Kent Kane, the heroic Arctic explorer, who died of the effects of his exposure in searching for Sir John Franklin and his ill-fated party. Mrs. Margaret Fox Kane has lately returned from England for a brief visit here, and she purposes in a very short time to deliver just one lecture, and no more, which shall shame and dumfound all the spiritualistic frauds who have not yet repented into poverty or exile of their nebulous ways. She will reveal one after another of the methods by which willing believers have been so briskly duped and robbed, and will herself demonstrate how simple, natural and easy are most of those methods.

Brooding upon the troubles that had been brought upon her by Spiritualism and on her personal guilt in connection with it, it is hardly strange that Mrs. Kane, even when bent upon making a sweeping confession of the whole imposture, should in intervals of nervous excitement have turned to the thought of suicide.

"'My troubles weighed upon me,' she said, 'and when I was coming over on the *Italy*, I do believe that I should have gone overboard but for the Captain and the doctor and some of the sailors. They prevented me, and when I landed, I could not express to them the gratitude I felt.

I had very little English money with me, but all of that I distributed to the men.'"

As Mrs. Kane told of her impulse to commit suicide her manner became tragic and she clutched her listener's arm. After a moment, however, she reverted quietly enough to the original subject.

But she speedily became much excited again, as what follows will show. It was but natural:

"Since you now despise Spiritualism, how was it that you were engaged in it so long?" I asked.

"Another sister of mine," and she coupled the name with an injurious adjective, "made me take up with it. She's my damnable enemy. I hate her. My God! I'd poison her! No, I wouldn't, but I'll lash her with my tongue. She was twenty-three years old the day I was born. I was an aunt seven years before I was born. Ha! ha!

"Yes, I am going to expose Spiritualism from its very foundation. I have had the idea in my head for many a year, but I have never come to a determination before. I've thought of it day and night. I loath the thing I have been. As I used to say to those who wanted me to give a séance, 'You are driving me into hell.' Then the next day I would drown my remorse in wine. I was too honest to remain a 'medium.' That's why I gave up my exhibitions.

"When Spiritualism first began Kate and I were little children, and this old woman, my other sister, made us her tools. Mother was a silly woman. She was a fanatic. I call her that because she was honest. She believed in these things. Spiritualism started from just nothing. We were but innocent little children. What did we know? Ah, we grew to know too much! Our sister used us in her exhibitions and we made money for her. Now she turns upon us because she's the wife of a rich man, and she opposes us both wherever she can. Oh, I am after her! You can kill sometimes without using weapons, you know.

"Dr. Kane found me when I was leading this life. [The woman's voice trembled just here and she nearly broke down.] I was only thirteen when he took me out of it and placed me at school. I was educated in Philadelphia. When I was sixteen years old he returned from the Arctic and we were married. Now comes the sad, sad tale. He was very ill. The physicians ordered him to London, but before he arrived he had a paralytic stroke of the heart. Then he was sent back from London and to Havana. Newsboys shouted in the streets of New York the news of his critical condition. Oh, my God! it was anguish to my ears! Mother and I were to have joined him in two weeks. He died before we arrived. Then I had brain fever. No one but God can know what sorrows I have had!

"When I recovered I was driven again into Spiritualism, and I gave exhibitions with my sister Katie. I knew, of course, then, that every effect produced by us was absolute fraud. Why, I have explored the unknown as far as human will can. I have gone to the dead so that I might get from them some little token. Nothing ever came of it—nothing, nothing. I have been in graveyards at dead of night, having permission to enter from those in charge. I have sat alone on a gravestone, that the spirits of those who slept underneath might come to me. I have tried to obtain some sign. Not a thing! No, no, the dead shall not return, nor shall any that go down into hell. So says the Catholic Bible, and so say I. The spirits will not come back. God has not ordered it.

"You want to know what are the points of my coming exposé? First the 'rappings.'"

Mrs. Kane paused here, and I heard first a rapping under the floor near my feet, then under the chair in which I was seated, and again under a table on which I was leaning. She led me to the door and I heard the same sound on the other side of it. Then, when she sat on the piano stool, the legs of the instrument reverberated more loudly, and the tap, tap, resounded throughout its hollow structure.

"It is all a trick?"

"Absolutely. Spirits, is he not easily fooled?"

Rap, rap, rap!

"I can always get an affirmative answer to that question," she remarked.

Then I addressed certain suppositions to her. At last she said, "Yes, you have hit it. It is, as you say, the manner in which the joints of the foot can be used without lifting it from the floor. The power of doing this can only be acquired by practice begun in early youth. One must begin as early as twelve years. Thirteen is rather late. We children, when we were playing together, years ago, discovered it, and it was my eldest sister who first put the discovery to such an infamous use.

"I call it infamous, for it was."

CHAPTER II.

THE DISCOMFITED ENEMY.

What has gone before is the whole story, in a sense.

The article in the *Herald* either relates or suggests it. Indeed, no refutation of it has been attempted. If there is one striking negative feature in the circumstances surrounding this exposure of Spiritualism, it is the entire absense of any reply from the great body of professional spiritualists commensurate with the accusation made.

This confession of Mrs. Margaret Fox Kane was to them the handwriting on the wall, the "*Mene, mene, tekel, upharsin,*" of Spiritualism.

Leah Fox Fish-Brown-Underhill, who has published a book of the flimsiest and most absurd narrative, intended to be accepted as a proof of

Spiritualism, is the one person in all the world who could be expected to defend the system from this fatal attack, if any defense were possible. Reporters of the daily press would have been but too glad to record whatever she might say, were it even the veriest drivel, on an issue that jeopardized the existence of the brazen and pretentious "ism" which, as by an obscene spell, still enlists the curiosity of a great proportion of the world.

But as Mrs. Underhill's book itself, which I shall notice more in detail hereafter, shows to the critical mind how futile would be an attempted refutation on her part, the public can very readily understand the reason of this most careful silence. Blunderingly, however, prior to having consulted her, Mr. Daniel Underhill, her husband, consented to talk upon the subject. The statements hostile to Mrs. Kane, to be found in the excerpt here given, were, of course, to be expected. Were they ever so true, however, they could not in any way lesson the damning force of her repentant avowals :—

Mr. Daniel Underhill, president of a wealthy insurance company, whose office is in Wall street, and who is the husband of the eldest of the Fox sisters, whom Margaret declares to be her "damnable enemy," is a Spiritualist, but in a moderate sense. Mrs. Underhill's maiden name was Ann Leah Fox. She was twice married before she met her present husband, and she is twenty-three years older than Margaret.

A large part of the public do not realize that Ann Leah, Margaret and Cathie Fox were the founders of what is specifically known as Spiritualism. The first so-called phenomena came to the two youngest girls in 1848, at Hydesville, in this State, while their sister Leah was residing elsewhere. When she heard of what had taken place and of the intense public excitement which it had created, she joined them, and then began the public history of Spiritualism. She took the incipient "ism" vigorously in hand, and for a series of years gave exhibitions in all the principal cities, which were attended by the most eminent men and the most brilliant women in the country.

Of late years Mrs. Underhill has entirely withdrawn

from public participation in spiritualistic exhibitions. She is still held, however, in high estimation by all who accept supernatural communications, and her reply to what her sister Margaret has said regarding the practice of fraud, would at this time be interesting. Unfortunately she is now in the country, and there is no person in the city to speak for her excepting her husband. I obtained an interview with him yesterday. He was reluctant to be brought into the controversy, but, while speaking in a most uncomplimentary manner of Margaret and denouncing her proposed new departure, did not evince any great amount of indignation.

"I have for years," he began, "helped both Maggie and Katie, and my wife has done everything in the world for them. We have furnished apartments for Maggie twice. They might both do well if they would only keep sober. Maggie can be as nice as you please or as vicious as a devil. Several persons have undertaken to manage her, but all have failed. Nobody can do anything with her. The first I knew that she was back in the city was through the *Herald*.

"I don't think she's in her right mind. I have done so much for her and she has behaved so badly in return that I have given her up now and will have nothing to do with her. She says she will lecture, does she? Well, I don't believe she ever will. She's incapable of it.

"It's a great pity, though, that she should say such things about Spiritualism, because of the odium which will result from it. But it isn't the first time she has said that she would declare against Spiritualism. She has had such spells before. It is astonishing to me that people have stuck to her and Katie as they have. It is all bosh about revealing the manner of producing the raps. I don't believe she can do it. I don't believe she knows how they are produced, except that it is done by an occult agency. Of course, there are frauds in Spiritualism. Mme. Diss De Barr was one of them. I don't believe much in materialization, but I've seen some real manifestations. They were in my own house. Nearly all my spiritualistic experience has been in my own house, and these sisters were the mediums.

"Of course Maggie's statement will be something of a shock to spiritualists the world over, because they regard her and her sisters as the founders of their belief. In my opinion she is not accountable for what she says."

Mrs. Underhill remained quietly in the country many weeks after the exposé, safe from the keen inquisition of reporters.

The notorious "mediums" in New York who were approached on the subject, were all excessively guarded in their comments upon the step taken by Mrs. Kane, yet they admitted her personal importance as an originator of Spiritualism. Mrs. E. A. Wells, whose fraudulent exhibitions have had a certain success, expressed herself as much shocked at the determination of Mrs. Kane; " 'but,' she added to the reporter, with seeming naîveté, 'you don't believe she will do it, do you?' "

The account from which I am quoting, continues as follows:

"I sought the presence of Mrs. E. A. Wells, a medium of great celebrity, whose abode is not far from Adelphi Hall, where spiritualists congregate on Sunday. Mrs. Wells expressed herself as shocked at the determination of Mrs. Margaret Fox Kane, "but," she added, with seeming naîveté, "you don't believe she will do it, do you?"

"How have you regarded Mrs. Kane heretofore, Mrs. Wells?"

"Why, with a good deal of respect as one of the first to get messages from the unseen world. The Fox sisters have a great name. I have no idea, though, if she really intends to do what she says she will, that she's in her right senses."

Another "medium," who has a wealthy clientèle, and who gives only private seances, whence all unfriendly influences are rigorously excluded, did not desire to appear in print, as she told her visitor, since it would look like "bad form" to those who came to her for supernatural enlightenment.

. She was asked, however, if she held the Fox sisters in much esteem as the pioneers of Spiritualism. She said she did, but personally knew nothing of them.

When told about the threatened exposure she expressed very great surprise, and declared that it would be a deep mortification to believers in Spiritualism.

"I don't believe she can expose any fraud. But if fraud exists, why, then, I say let it be exposed; the sooner the better. There's no fraud about me, that's very certain, and I've some of the very best people in New York to come here."

"I'll tell you what! I have heard that the Fox sisters are dreadfully addicted to drink. I don't know how far it is true, but I wouldn't believe anything she might say in the way of exposure. May be she's out of money and thinks the spiritualists ought to do something for her. I shouldn't wonder."

"Now, if you'll come up here some time, and if you'll give me a fair report, I shall be glad to show you how I can materialize."

I thought there was a good deal of material about her already, and so I thanked her.

At their public gatherings in Adelphi Hall, New York, now most meagerly attended, the spiritualists, just after the initial exposé in the *Herald*, refrained very wisely from taking up the gauntlet of truth thrown down by their chief apostle, Mrs. Margaret Fox Kane. In an interview, however, which was had by a reporter with Mr. Henry J. Newton, the President of the First Spiritual Society of New York, the latter indulged in a number of emphatic statements regarding the "manifestations" produced by the "Fox Sisters," all of which rested upon his own veracity only. The spirit of what he said may be easily gleaned from this passage :

"I had supposed all along," he said, "that Mrs. Kane was still in Europe, and that she would never return to this country. I even heard at the time when Katie, her sister, was sent abroad, that Maggie was in Rome, in company with a well known gentleman. I am very much surprised to know that she is in this city, and more surprised that she threatens to make such silly pretended revelations as you say she proposes. They can only be revelations in name. She cannot reveal anything that can injure the spiritualist cause or that will weaken in any one's mind the truth of what we teach.

"I have been absent in the country and have not read all that the *Herald* has published on this matter. I have read enough, however, to show me how utterly absurd and ridiculous her position is.

"The idea of claiming that unseen ' rappings ' can be produced with joints of the feet ! If she says this, even with regard to her own manifestations, she lies ! I and many other men of truth and position have witnessed the manifestations of herself and her sisters many times under circumstances in which it was absolutely impossible for there to have been the least fraud.

"*Nothing that she could say in that regard would in the least change my opinion,* nor would it that of any one else who has become profoundly convinced that there is an occult influence connecting us with an invisible world,

I have seen Margaret Fox Kane herself, when lying on a bed of sickness and unable to rise, produce 'rappings' in various parts of the room in which she was, and upon the ceilings, doors and windows several feet away from her. I have seen her produce the same effects when too drunk to realize what she was doing."

On the 25th of September, 1888, the following, which was published in the New York *Herald*, expressed very tersely the situation among the spiritualists, who had by that time partly recovered from the first effect of the blow:

Recrimination against the two younger Fox sisters, Margaret and Katie, has begun with characteristic violence, and many unlovely truths are betrayed which do not alter the essential significance of the former's denunciation of spiritualistic fraud. Several of the mediums said that they could hardly believe their eyes when they read of Mrs. Margaret Fox Kane's determination, and they declared almost unanimously that "she would not do it if she were in her senses." They accuse her of excessive indulgence in drink and hint that she is not responsible for what she says. It appears, however, that in private, on many occasions, but never before in public, she has stated that Spiritualism was a tissue of fraud, and that some day she would prove the charge to the world. She has during the last few months given many séances in London, but always disclaimed any personal supernatural connection in producing the effects at which others wondered. With a number of rich patrons, among them Mr. H. Wedgewood, of Cavendish Square, she proceeded to a certain point in the process of delusion and then frankly undeceived them, convincing them of the ease with which they could be practiced upon.

Prior to this, the following had been published:

As Mrs. Kane's sincerity in making her proposed exposures is questioned by her enemies, the following brief note from a well known English spiritualist is of interest:

"31 QUEEN ANNE STREET, CAVENDISH SQUARE,
"LONDON, W., JULY 19, 1888.

"DEAR MRS. KANE: I am not so much surprised as I might be at what you have revealed to me if I had not already been led to believe that many spiritualistic mediums practice upon the credulous.

"The illusion, however, was perfect while it lasted.

"You do well to expose these infamous frauds, and I thank you for having enlightened me.

"Sincerely yours,

"H. WEDGEWOOD."

And later Mrs. Kane, in outlining her proposed public lecture, said :

"I am going to expose the very root of corruption in this spiritualistic ulcer. You talk about Mormonism! Do you know that there is something behind the shadowy mask of Spiritualism that the public can hardly guess at? I am stating now what I know, not because I actually participated in it, for I would never be a party to such promiscuous nastiness, but because I had plenty of opportunity, as you may imagine, of verifying it. Under the name of this dreadful, this horrible hypocrisy —Spiritualism—everything that is improper, bad and immoral is practiced. They go even so far as to have what they call 'spiritual children!' They pretend to something like the immaculate conception! Could anything be more blasphemous, more disgusting, more thinly deceptive than that? In London I went in disguise to a quiet séance at the house of a wealthy man, and I saw a so-called materialization. The effect was produced with the aid of luminous paper, the lustre of which was reflected upon the operator. The figure thus displayed was that of a woman—was virtually nude, being enveloped in transparent gauze, the face alone being concealed. This was one of those séances to which the privileged non-believing friends of believing spiritualists could have access. But there are other séances, where none but the most tried and trusted are admitted, and where there are shameless goings on that vie with the secret Saturnalia of the Romans. I could not describe these things to you, because I would not."

Thus, the only one of the "Fox Sisters" who still adhered to the imposture practiced for over forty years, and the only spiritualist who could deny the statements of Margaret Fox Kane with anything approaching to authority, found her safest and most fitting defense in the kindly shelter of silence.

This quasi-confession was not needed to complete the conviction in intelligent minds that

Spiritualism was, in its inception, and is now, a fraud and a lie. But the significance of the negative circumstance is none the less worthy of note.

CHAPTER III.

A SECOND BLOW.

Barely had the professional spiritualists a breathing-spell—after the shock of Mrs. Kane's confession—when a new blow fell upon them.

Mrs. Catherine Fox Jencken arrived from Europe, and though ignorant until landing, of the grave step her sister Margaret had taken, at once announced her intention of joining and sustaining her in the complete exposure of Spiritualism in all its phases of deception and hypocrisy.

This news staggered the spiritualistic world.

And now it but remains for the other of the three "Fox Sisters" to see the hopeless folly of continued imposture, and to add her confession to the historical record of the dissipation of this unholy fraud. That she will ever do this, however, those who are aware that to her malevolent will was due the first evil growth and the wide extension of Spiritualism, cannot easily bring themselves to believe.

The following account of Mrs. Jencken's arrival in New York and of her determination to add her testimony to that of her sister Margaret against the fraud of Spiritualism, was published on the 10th of October, 1888, and is of sufficient interest to excuse my quoting it here at large :

AND KATY FOX NOW.

The Youngest of the Mediumistic Pioneers Will "Give the Snap Away."

SHE ARRIVES FROM EUROPE.

Spiritualism a Humbug from Beginning to End—Alleged Immoralities.

Katie Fox Jencken arrived yesterday from England on the *Persian Monarch* and she intends to co-operate

A SECOND BLOW.

with her sister—Margaret Fox Kane—in her proposed exposé of the fraudulent methods of so-called Spiritualism.

Mrs. Jencken's coming was unexpected to her sister, and it will surprise the enemies of both.

The blow to Spiritualism which Maggie Fox struck not long ago, caused a good deal more of consternation than spiritualists generally have cared to confess. There is ample reason for stating that underneath a plausible surface of enforced calm there have been the hurried exchange of forbodings and doubtings, and many consultations and goings to and fro. It is known that an overture was made to Maggie Fox suggestive of a money consideration for her silence, and that she rejected it with much indignation.

Mrs. Jencken walked into the parlor where Mrs. Kane was sitting about five o'clock yesterday, and the sisters at once fell on each other's necks, in an ecstasy of affection and delight at being together once again. Mrs. Kane had but just been talking to me about her projected lecture on "The Curse of Spiritualism," and Mrs. Jencken, who had heard nothing of the proposed exposé, except as it was casually rumored in her ear at the steamship dock, promptly gave her acquiescence to it as soon as she understood the situation.

"I do not care a fig for Spiritualism," she said,

"except so far as the good will of its adherents may affect the future of my boys. They are all I have in this life, and I live or die for them."

Mrs. Jencken looks a far different person than she was when in deep trouble in this city and when she had to do with the rather unsympathetic measures of the Society for the Prevention of Cruelty to Children. No matron could bear a more placid and comely expression, and she declares with heartfelt earnestness that she is done forever with her once-besetting vice.

"Mrs. Jencken, are you willing to join with your sister in exposing the true modus operandi of Spiritualism?" I asked.

"I care nothing for Spiritualism," was her reply. "So far as I am concerned I am done with it. I will say this, I regard it as one of the very greatest curses that the world has ever known. If I knew those powerful spiritualists who have done their utmost to harm me in the past could not do so in the future, I would not hesitate a moment to expose it. The worst of them all is my eldest sister, Leah, the wife of Daniel Underhill. I think she was the one who caused my arrest last spring, and the bringing of the preposterous charge against me that I was cruel to my children and neglectful of them. I don't know why it is, she has always been jealous of

Maggie and me; I suppose because we could do things in Spiritualism that she couldn't."

"Why don't you come squarely out, then, with the truth, and make the public your friends? You needn't fear any persecution if you do that."

"Well, if my sister's health were only fully restored and I knew she was fully herself I would certainly join her in showing Spiritualism to be what it really is. I want to be sure of that, however. I want the thing done properly when it is done."

"Then you will not deny that what she has said of Spiritualism is true?"

"I will not deny it. Spiritualism is a humbug from beginning to end. It is the greatest humbug of the century. I don't know whether she has told you this, but Maggie and I started it as very little children, too young, too innocent, to know what we were doing. Our sister Leah was twenty-three years older than either of us. We got started in the way of deception, and being encouraged in it, we went on, of course. Others, old enough to have been ashamed of the infamy, took us out into the world. My sister Leah has published a book called 'The Missing Link of Spiritualism.' It professes to give the true history of this movement, so far as it originated with us. Now, there's nothing but falsehood in that book from beginning to end, excepting the fact that Horace Greeley educated me. The rest is nothing but a string of lies."

"And about the manifestations at Hydesville in 1848 and the finding of bones in the cellar and so on ?"

"All humbuggery, every bit of it."

"And yet Maggie and I are the founders of Spiritualism!" concluded Mrs. Jencken.

On the next day Mrs. Jencken made the statement which appears in the following:

Mrs. Jencken was asked about the alleged spirit manifestations which have taken place in Carlyle's old home at Chelsea, London, where she has lately resided. The English papers have been filled with stories, more or less sceptical, regarding these queer occurrences. Mrs. Jencken said: "All that took place there of that nature is utterly false. I haven't the slightest idea that the noises which we heard in the house had any connection with Carlyle's spirit. I certainly know that every so-called manifestation produced through me in London or anywhere else was a fraud. Many a time have I wept because when I was young and innocent I was brought into such a life. The time has now come for Maggie and I to set ourselves right before the world. Nobody knows at what moment either of us might be taken away. We ought not to leave this base fabric of deceit behind us unexposed."

As may be seen, nothing could be stronger than the language employed in these interviews by both of the repentant sisters, in denouncing their former adhesion to a system of humbug and hypocrisy.

CHAPTER IV.

THE HAND OF THE PERSECUTOR

The public had every reason to feel a deep sympathy with the two younger Fox sisters in the courageous attitude which they had taken.

The deadliest hatred is always to be feared, by those who abandon a faith or a system, from those who still adhere to it.

Think you, if Mahomet had turned about, forty years after the Hegira, and had boldly anathematized the religion he had established, he might not have been reviled and persecuted, even by those in whom he had first inculcated his bastard faith?

Who can doubt this who knows human nature?

Even the lies of an impostor rebel against

him, when, with a repentant word, he would damn them again to all eternity.

Mrs. Jencken had ample reason to fear that the disclosures which had been made by her and her sister would redouble the hostile zeal of those who before had persecuted her. In the first account which had been published of her return to this country, it was not stated that her two boys had accompanied her. In fact, however, they had.

The pressure brought to bear to induce her to retract her denunciation of Spiritualism, and the ground of her fear for the safety of her children, are well set forth in the following, which appeared on October 11th, 1888:

FEARING THEIR ENEMIES.

THE JENCKEN BOYS WERE HERE, BUT ARE SENT AWAY.

There are signs of gathering thunder all around the spirtualistic sky.

A leading spiritualist, a lawyer, who had read the *Herald's* recent articles on the subject, demanded of Mrs. Katy Fox Jencken, immediately upon her arrival in New York on Tuesday, that she refuse to support her sister Maggie in her exposé of mediumistic fraud, and, to use his own words, that she "throw herself upon the sympathy of the spiritualists."

This proposition she emphatically rejected and declared that she had done forever with Spiritualism and spiritualists. She firmly believes that leading men and women among the latter, particularly her eldest sister Leah, are her secret persecutors, and that it was due to their animus that she was arrested last spring and deprived of her two boys, to whom she is immeasurably devoted.

There is much to sustain this charge, and the inference that this mysterious persecution, of which, as she alleges, the Society for the Prevention of Cruelty to Children was only the intrument, was inspired by the fear that she and Mrs. Kane, having long been exploited for the financial benefit of others, might do the very thing they are doing now—betray the secrets of deception, which have from the beginning of the spiritualistic movement been so well guarded.

As was said in the *Herald* yesterday, Mrs. Jencken knew nothing of the course which her sister Maggie had taken until she landed on the wharf of the Monarch line company. The *Herald* did not state yesterday that Mrs. Jencken was accompanied by her two boys, whom the Society for the Prevention of Cruelty to Children made such great efforts to keep apart from their mother in last May. As soon as she heard the news of Maggie's disclosures from a friend who met her at the steamer, she was overcome with fear lest, being now aware of the means that had been employed to secure their release and her own, the society would again attempt to deprive her of her children. She was advised by a lawyer who knew the real source of the hostility to her and the motives that prompted it, to send them back at once to England. The boys declared that they did not want to fall into the hands of the Society for the Prevention of Cruelty to Children again. Both of them are now strapping big fellows for their age, and are able and willing to earn their own living. One is fourteen years old and the other will be soon sixteen. But for a misunderstanding as to their ages on the part of the police justice last spring there would never have been any question of retaining them in the custody of Mr. Gerry's over-zealous myrmidons.

Mrs. Jencken's apprehensions, however, were not to be quieted, and early in the morning she bundled off the two lads [and they are now safely beyond the jurisdiction of the dreaded society of which Mr. E. T. Gerry is the chief].*

"This shows," said a gentleman yesterday, "how far certain wealthy spiritualists are powerful to inspire a kind of terrorism even in New York city among those who have left their ranks."

"Now that my boys are out of danger," said Mrs. Jencken, "I will stand by my sister Maggie and go to the very fullest length of any exposure that she may make. We have been the tools and victims of others long enough. I approve and I affirm all that she has said about the immoral practices hidden under the ridiculous cloak of Spiritualism. The whole thing is damnable, and it should long ago have been trampled out as one would trample out the life of a serpent."

* It was erroneously stated that the boys were immediately sent back to Europe.

CHAPTER V.

SOLEMN ABJURATION.

The news that Mrs. Margaret Fox Kane and Mrs. Catherine Fox Jencken had renounced and exposed Spiritualism, flew from one end of the country to the other, and caused excitement among spiritualists and non-spiritualists. Every newspaper in every city of the United States, and many in Europe, repeated the story published in New York.

The general opinion everywhere, where the wish was not the opposite, was that Spiritualism as such had received its death-blow.

Letters began to pour in upon Mrs. Kane which were strongly significant of the effect of her action. Many of them were written by persons who had been believers from the very first of the public exhibitions of the "rappings," and who had based their whole faith on the truth and veritable inspiration of the "Fox Sisters." It was almost pitiable to witness the honest-hearted distress of people of this sort, who now saw the fondest illusion of their lives dissolve before their eyes; their dearest, assured hope of an invisible world ruthlessly torn from them.

The anger of those who now anathematized the founders of the spiritualistic faith, and declared that all that they could now say in way of recantation was utterly false, while all that they had formerly said or performed as miraculous proof, was, of course, as true as gospel, or as the fact that the sun shines, was quite as ridiculous as the other sentiment was worthy of sympathy.

It was natural that those who had fed their baser passions upon Spiritualism—as the harpy upon carrion—should resort to the vilest methods of attacking Mrs. Kane, and in doing so should shelter themselves behind the cowardly refuge of anonymity.

A single communication from one of those who thus set the gauge for our estimate of spiritualistic hypocrisy, will suffice to complete the reader's impression regarding them. It was written on a postal card and unsigned, and the italics and other literary peculiarities are wholly those of the person who wrote it:

"Mrs. Kane. Your anticipated action Thursday night reminds me *very forcibly* of several lines of 'Beautiful snow' only your Course is even *more despicable* and your rank in the history of the present day will be on a par with Benedict arnold In 'Beautiful Snow' we find 'Selling her soul to whoever would buy' &c. you are going to sell your soul to an ignorant public by *pretending* to *Expose* what *you very well Know cannot be Exposed* by any man, woman or child dwelling in the Mortal sphere of Life—shame on you. but you will soon meet your reward in other spheres and suffer for your wickedness."

It is hard to determine whether the above communication emanated from a professional spiritualist of the mercenary type or from one who finds his or her profit of self-gratification in the licentious tendencies and opportunities of private spiritualistic intercourse. In any event, it bears the stamp of ignorant selfishness and narrow vulgarity.

It is with a degree of pleasure that one may turn to letters which were written by the sincere disciples of the "Fox Sisters," and which breathe a deep anxiety for the fate of that fantastic creed in which they have so much delighted.

The reader has but to think for an instant of the actual meaning of this long-deferred exposé to these persons. They had greedily fed their souls upon the delusion that they had held intercourse with the spirits of their dear departed. The supposed messages which they had received seemed a sure earnest of that union with those they loved on earth for which the true heart most longs. In view of this expectation and in the light of this exposure of its utter fallacy—so far as any material evidence is concerned—it is most difficult to find adequate terms with which to characterize the work of those who still persist in contributing to a delusion which has numbered so many victims.

Here is a letter from a resident of Southern California, enclosing a clipping from a newspaper containing Mrs. Kane's renunciation of Spiritualism:

"BUENA PARK, LOS ANGELES CO., CAL.,
SEPT. 29, A. D. 1888.
"MRS. MARGARET FOX KANE,
"DEAR MADAM:
"I have just read the enclosed item, taken from one of our Los Angeles city papers. Please let me know if the statements therein contained are true, and you will greatly oblige,
"Yours for truth,
"T. J. HOUSE."

The following was written by one of the best known early settlers of San Francisco, a man whose example and absolute faith have influenced hundreds, probably, to embrace Spiritualism:

"SAN FRANCISCO, CAL., OCT. 2, 1888.
"MRS. MARGARET FOX KANE,
"DEAR MADAM:

"I inclose a cutting from one of our local papers, purporting to be an interview with you in regard to the subject of Spiritualism. I have taken the liberty to inquire of you if the statements therein contained are true.

"I have been a believer in the phenomena from its first inception through you and your sister, believing it to be true since that time.

"I am now eighty-one years old and have but a short time, of course, to remain in this world, and I feel great anxiety to know through you if I have been deceived all this time in a matter of vital interest to us all.

"Will you greatly oblige me with an answer?
"Very respectfully yours,
"E. F. BUNNELL.
"No. 319 Kearny St."

And here is a communication which is signed by what is evidently only a part of the writer's name, but which carries with it in every line the absolute impress of truth and of a deep and pathetic earnestness :

"Boston, Mass., Oct. 15, 1888.
"Mrs. Margaret Fox Kane,
"Dear Madam :
"Hundreds of thousands have believed through you and you alone. Hundreds of thousands eagerly ask you whether all the glorious light that they fancied you have given them, was but the false flicker of a common dip-candle of fraud.

"If, as you say, you were forced to pursue this imposture from childhood, I can forgive you, and I am sure that God will ; for he turns not back the truly repentant. I will not upbraid you. I am sure you have suffered as much as any penalty, human or divine, could cause you to suffer. The disclosures that you make take from me all that I cherished most. There is nothing left for me now but to hope for the reality of that repose which death promises us.

"It is perhaps better that the delusion should be at last swept away by one single word, and that word 'fraud.'

"I know that the pursuit of this shadowy belief has wrought upon my brain and that I am no longer my old self. Money I have spent in thousands and thousands of dollars within a few short years to propitiate the 'mediumistic' intelligence. It is true that never once have I received a message or the token of a word that did not leave a still unsatisfied longing in my heart, a feeling that it was not really my loved one after all, who was speaking to me, or if it was my loved one, that he was changed, that I hardly knew him and that he hardly knew me. Oh! how I have hated the thought that used to come to me sometimes, in spite of myself, that it was not really he. But that must have been the true intuition. It is better that the delusion is past, after all, for had I kept on in that way, I am sure I should have gone mad. The constant seeking, the frequent pretended response, its unsatisfying meaning, the sense of distance and change between me and my loved one—oh! it has been horrible, horrible!

"He who is dying of thirst and has the sweet cup ever snatched from his lips, just as the first drop touches them—he alone can know what in actual things is the similitude of this spiritualistic torture.

"God bless you, for I think that you now speak the truth. You have my forgiveness at least, and I believe that thousands of others will forgive you, for the atonement made in season wipes out much of the stain of the early sin.

"Yours sincerely,
"ANNA SUZANNE."

To these letters and to hundreds of others which Mrs. Kane and her sister Mrs. Jencken have received, this volume is their response.

But besides this, they have appeared in public on the platform, as an earnest of their present sincerity, and will probably continue so to appear in various parts of this country and Europe.

On the 21st of October, 1888, Mrs. Margaret Fox Kane first fulfilled her intention of publicly denouncing, with her own lips, Spiritualism and its attendant trickery. She appeared at the Academy of Music in New York before a large and distinguished audience, and without reservation demonstrated the falsity of all that she had done in the past in the guise of spiritualistic "mediumship."

The ordeal was a severe one. The great nervous strain under which she had labored rendered her mind highly excitable, and the large number of spiritualists in the house tried to create a disturbance, or a traitorous diversion which would break the force of her renunciation. In this they utterly failed, however, thanks to the superior character of a majority of her auditors.

The moral effect of the exposure could not have been greater.

Mrs. Kane stood before the footlights trembling with intense feeling, and made the following most solemn abjuration of Spiritualism, while Mrs. Catharine Fox Jencken sat in a neighboring box and gave assent by her presence to all that she said :

"That I have been chiefly instrumental in prepetrating the fraud of Spiritualism upon a too confiding public, most of you doubtless know.

"The greatest sorrow of my life has been that this is true, and though it has come late in my day, I am now prepared to tell the truth, the whole truth and nothing but the truth,—so help me God!

"There are probably many here who will scorn me for the deception I have practiced, yet did they know the true history of my unhappy past, the living agony and shame that it has been to me, they would pity, not reproach.

"The imposition which I have so long maintained began in my early childhood, when, with character and mind still unformed, I was unable to distinguish between right and wrong.

"I repented it in my maturity. I have lived through years of silence, through intimidation, scorn and bitter adversity, concealing as best I might, the consciousness of my guilt. Now, thanks to God and my awakened conscience, I am at last able to reveal the fatal truth, the exact truth of this hideous fraud which has withered so many hearts and has blighted so many hopeful lives.

"I am here to-night as one of the founders of Spiritualism, to denounce it as an absolute falsehood from beginning to end, as the flimsiest of superstitions, the most wicked blasphemy known to the world.

"I ask only your kind attention and forgiveness, and as I may prove myself worthy by the step I am now taking, may you extend to me your helping hands and sustain me in the better path I have chosen."

The demonstration of the method by which the "rappings" were produced was a perfect success, as is best shown by the following succinct account, which formed a part of the article on the subject published by the New York *World* on the following morning:

A plain wooden stool or table, resting upon four short legs, and having the properties of a sounding board, was placed in front of her. Removing her shoe, she placed her right foot upon this table. The entire house became breathlessly still, and was rewarded by a number of little short, sharp raps—those mysterious sounds which have for more than forty years frightened and bewildered hundreds of thousands of people in this country and Europe. A committee, consisting of three physicians taken from the audience, then ascended to the stage, and having made an examination of her foot during the progress of the "rappings," unhesitatingly agreed that the sounds were made by the action of the first joint of her large toe.

Only the most hopelessly prejudiced and bigoted fanatics of Spiritualism could withstand the irresistable force of this common-place explanation and exhibition of how "spirit rappings" are produced. The demonstration was perfect and complete, and if "spirit rappings" find any credence in this community hereafter, it would seem a wise precaution on the part of the authorities to begin the enlargement of the State's insane asylums without any delay.

III.
HISTORY.

CHAPTER VI.

ORIGIN OF THE FRAUD.

There are spiritualists who pretend that so-called "spirit rappings" originated long before the Hydesville disturbances took place. These declarations, however, are of no value as actual evidence.

In any event, there is no claim that in their cause and general character these manifestations, so-called, were very different from similar ones of the present day.

The "rappings" produced by the "Fox Sisters" are certainly the first of which there is an authentic account. They began in a little rustic cottage at a place called Hydesville, in the town of Arcadia, near Newark, Wayne County, New

York. Here John D. Fox and his wife Margaret dwelt with their two daughters, Margaret and Catherine. Two other children, Ann Leah and David S., lived elsewhere. There was sometimes a fifth member of the household, also a child. This was Elizabeth Fish, the daughter of Leah, and therefore the niece of Margaret and Catherine. She was seven years older than the elder of the two latter.

The elder Fox and his wife had not been always united since their marriage. They were separated for a number of years. The three older children, Ann Leah, Maria and David S., were conceived before this separation took place, and Margaret and Catherine afterwards. The two broods had distinctive characteristics. The father, in the interval, is said to have become addicted to intemperate habits. The taint of heredity may excuse much in the younger generation that sprang from a weakness of will-power and made them the too easy victims of colder and more mercenary natures. To many it is well known that they are still incapable of guarding their interests in a business way, and that they have always been too largely at the mercy of any one who could acquire an influence over them.

Margaretta, or Margaret, Fox, as she always signs herself, was born in the year 1840, and Catherine Fox a year and a half later. The eldest sister Leah was born twenty-three years before the former. The little girls, one eight years old and the other six and a half, had rarely seen this sister prior to the beginning of the spiritualistic movement. She knew nothing of it until the popular excitement over the "rappings" had almost reached its climax. Very early in life she had married a man named Fish, who had deserted her, and she was supporting herself at this time in the city of Rochester by teaching the rudiments of music. David S. Fox, son of John and Margaret Fox, lived about two miles from the home of his father in Arcadia.

Maggie and Katie Fox were as full of petty devilment as any two children of their age ever were. They delighted to tease their excellent old mother, who by all who knew her is described as simple, gentle and true-hearted. In their antics, they would resort to all sorts of ingenious devices, and bed-time witnessed almost invariably the gayest of larks. One of their frequent amusements was to plague their niece, Elizabeth, who slept in the same bed with them, by kicking and tickling her, and by frightening her at almost any hour of the night out of sound sleep.

Their riotous fancy soon hit upon the plan of bobbing apples up and down on the floor in their bedchamber, as a means of scaring Elizabeth and of puzzling their mother without much risk of detection. They tied strings to the stems of the apples, and thus let them hang down beside the bed. The noise of dropping them more or less quickly upon the floor resembled almost anything that the imagination chose to liken it to, from raps on the front door to slippered foot-falls on the narrow stairway. Whenever a search was made for the cause of the noises, the apples were easily hauled up into the bed and hidden in the bedclothes, where no one would think of looking for them, at least at that stage of the investigation.

The plan had everything in it to charm a juvenile mischief-maker. It succeeded admirably. It was not till the wonder which was caused by these strange "knockings" had extended beyond the humble Fox household, that the suggestion of any other means of affording to that growing feeling its daily food of seeming evidence came to the roguish youngsters.

The family had moved into the house at Hydesville on December 11, 1847. The mother began to hear strange sounds almost from that date—strange because they occurred with great frequency and were oddly repeated. The children slept in what was called the East Room; the parents in an adjoining chamber. At all hours of the night, almost, the sounds were heard; but it happened that they always occurred when one or both of the children were wide awake. The mother, in a statement which has been published as one of the so-called proofs of the genuineness of these manifestations, says that the sounds could with difficulty be located. "Sometimes it seemed as if the furniture was moved; but on examination we found everything in order. The children had become so alarmed that I thought best to have them sleep in the room with us. * * * On the night of the first disturbance we all got up and lighted a candle and searched the house, the noises continuing during the time, and being heard near the same place."

How natural it was that little children, being averse to sleeping away from their elders in a dark room in a lone country neighborhood, should take advantage of a pretext such as this to get their bed placed nearer to that of their parents! Such, indeed, was the immediate result.

The third night of the "rappings" was the 31st of March, 1848. Mrs. Fox says:

"*The children who slept in the other bed in*

the room heard the rappings and tried to make similar sounds with their fingers.

"Katie exclaimed :

"'Mr. Splitfoot,' (the imaginary person who was supposed to make the noises), 'do as I do ;' clapping her hands. The sound instantly followed her with the same number of raps ; when she stopped, the sound ceased for a short time. Then Margaret said in sport : 'Now, do just as I do ; count one, two, three, four,' striking one hand against the other at the same time, and the raps came as before. * * * I then thought I could put a test that no one in the place could answer. I asked the noises to rap my children's ages, successively. Instantly, each one of my children's ages was given correctly, pausing between them sufficiently long to individualize them until the seventh, at which a longer pause was made, and then three more emphatic raps were given, corresponding to the age of the little one that died, which was my youngest child. I then asked : 'Is this a human being that answers my questions so correctly?' There was no rap. I asked: 'Is it a spirit? If so, make two raps,' which were instantly given as soon as the request was made. I then said: 'If it is an injured spirit, make two raps,' which were instantly made, causing the house to tremble. I asked: 'Were you injured in this house?' The answer was given as before. 'Is the person living that injured you?' Answer by raps in the same manner. I ascertained by the same method that it was a man, aged thirty-one years; that he had been murdered in this house; and his remains were buried in the cellar; that his family consisted of a wife and five children, two sons and three daughters, all living at the time of his death, but that his wife had since died."

Then the supposed spirit was asked if it would continue to "rap" if the neighbors were called in to listen. The answer was affirmative.

And so they were called in.

This caused the commencement of that great excitement which so soon spread from neighborhood to village, from the village to the near-by city of Rochester, and thence all over the country.

Mrs. Margaret Fox Kane says at the present time :

"The apple-dropping trick appeared to us small children so simple and innocent, that we could only wonder that any one attached so great an importance to the sounds we produced. Only think of our ages at that time, and then ask, if you will, how we could have even the shade of a realization of the real meaning of this deception !

"This lying book of Mrs. Underhill's, notwithstanding its abominable object, does give some slight inkling of the truth here and there.

"It is thus that the wicked confound themselves.

"She quotes, as you see here, what she says to be my mother's words : 'The children who slept in the other bed in the room, heard the rapping and tried to make similar sounds by snapping their fingers.'

"Now that is really just how we first got the idea of producing with the joints similar sounds to those we had made by dropping apples with a string. From trying it with our fingers we then tried it with our feet, and it did not take long for us to find out that we could easily produce very loud raps by the action of the toe-joints when in contact with any substance which is a good conductor of sound. My sister Katie was the first to discover that we could make such peculiar noises with our fingers. We used to practice first with one foot and then the other, and finally we got so we could do it with hardly an effort.

"Of course, I was so young then that many incidents have escaped my memory. I assert positively, however, that much of the effect of the 'rappings' is greatly exaggerated in this statement which my mother was made to write. I say that she was *made* to write it, because the wording of the statement, if not largely dictated by others in the first place—men who desired to make public the details of the 'rappings' and to make money by the sale of a pamphlet describing them—was afterwards grossly garbled, that it might be used to suit the dishonest purposes of professional spiritualists. I am not even certain that mother ever signed the document, of which Mrs. Underhill makes such great parade. The same is true regarding the other pieces of so-called evidence in her work. Utterly futile as they are, when confronted with my living testimony, and when judged by their own internal weakness, I should not regard them as in any sense genuine unless I could see the original handwriting and could recognize the signatures. I say to you now, that professional spiritualists are capable of going to any lengths to bolster up their impostures. No forgery, so long as there was the least chance of its succeeding, as a furtherance to their object, would in the least repel them. Some of the so-called statements in Leah's book I believe were manufactured from beginning to end, though to tell you the truth I have avoided reading the greater part of it because of the disgust I have felt for a long time for that whole infamous system of pretense and falsehood.

"Well, we were led on unintentionally by my good mother in the perpetration of this great wrong. She used to say when we were sitting in a dark circle at home: 'Is this a disembodied spirit that has taken possession of my dear children?' And then we would 'rap' just for the fun of the thing, you know, and mother would declare that it was the spirits that were speaking.

"Soon it went so far, and so many persons had heard the 'rappings' that we could not confess the wrong without exciting very great anger on the part of those we had deceived. So we went right on.

"It is wonderful, indeed, how two little children could have made this discovery, and how, by simply obeying the natural thirst for the marvelous, in others, and their inherent superstition, they should have advanced step by step, in the fraud, deluding those who most ardently wished to be deluded.

"Until first suggested to us by our mother, who was perfectly innocent in her belief, the thought of 'spirits' had never entered our heads. We were too young and too simple to imagine such a thing."

CHAPTER VII.

GARBLED AND DISTORTED TESTIMONY.

So the neighbors were called in at the Hydesville house and the "rappings" were continued.

By diligent questioning on the part of the older persons in the Fox household and of the neighbors, the mysterious noises were made to affirm or to deny almost anything which was suggested to the "mediums," often in accordance with knowledge that, it had been believed, was only possessed by a few persons.

And so the wonder grew, day by day.

Pursuing the idea that a man had been murdered in the house, the whole of a very horrible history was obtained, and the name even of the supposed murderer was indicated by affimative "raps" when mentioned together with others in a tentative way. The occupation of the victim was said to be that of a pedler. He had $500 in money and was buried in the creek which ran past the house.

Mrs. Underhill admits that some of the neighbors were misled and went to digging in the creek, called Ganargua, the water of which was then very low. But they speedily recognized the absurdity of this undertaking, and the girls, Maggie, Katie and Lizzie laughed at them for their pains. The bones of an old horse were found there and nothing more.

By this time the two sisters had arrived at very great proficiency in producing the raps. Such a crude and easily detected means as the bobbing of apples on the floor was early discarded. Often in the morning, before they dressed, and after the old folks had left their room, the sisters would stand in their bare feet on the floor and vie with each other in the laughable exercise of making the "strange" noises. It was impossible, of course, that Lizzie should not know the whole truth, although being about thirteen years old at this time, she was unabled to imitate the "raps" very successfully. Indeed, it is said that she was too frank and outspoken in disposition to engage long in any deception. When the children persisted in deluding their mother, partly for their amusement and partly because they were ashamed to retract what had already caused so much excitement and had drawn so much attention to themselves, Lizzie used to break out indignantly:

"*Now, Maggie, how can you say that it was done by spirits! You know yourself that it's all a story. It's a great shame to pretend such things.*"

Many occurrences of this description I have gathered from Mrs. Kane.

But Mrs. Leah Underhill, in her jumbled up narrative, states that "*When the raps broke out suddenly close to some of the family, or at the table, one of the girls would accuse the other of having caused them, saying, 'Now you did that, etc., etc.'*"

Thanks to Mrs. Leah Underhill, such hints of

the true explanation of these "manifestations" are plentiful throughout her book, and one needs only to bring some little intelligence to bear upon it to read between the lines the whole story of the fraud.

And here let me quote a passage which only goes to show how very strong was the love of deviltry in the children:

"Father had always been a regular Methodist in good standing, and was invariable in his practice of morning prayers; and *when he would be kneeling upon his chair, it would sometimes amuse the children to see him open wide his eyes as knocks would sound and vibrate on his chair itself.* He expressed it graphically to mother: 'When I am done praying that jigging stops.'"

Mrs. Margaret Fox Kane distinctly remembers incidents like this one; only she qualifies the narrative by saying that her father never opened his eyes when these annoyances came while he was at prayer, but went devoutly on to the end without heeding them,

How absurd for any one to suppose that if these sounds were produced by a cause unknown to the children, they would laugh at them and regard them as very great sport, instead of trembling and crying with affright!

"The sounds which were heard at those times," says Mrs. Kane in her statement to the writer, "were all produced by Katie and myself, and by no other being or spirit under the sun. Nor did we always do it with our feet. Frequently in that early stage of the excitement about the 'rappings,' we would make the sounds with our fingers, provided it was easy to do so without causing suspicion. In order to do it unknown to any one, we would sit with one hand hidden by an elbow resting upon the table, or the woodwork of a chair.

"Of course, our mother in her earnest belief, poor soul, excited us to do a great deal more than otherwise we would had done. The mystery of the sounds absorbed her entire being for the time. She became pale and worn-looking and thought that great misfortunes were to happen, and prayed often and fervently. I can well remember how my heart used to smite me at times when I looked upon her and knew that Katie and I were the cause of all her trouble. In later years, long after I had come to the age of understanding, I had very bitter reasons for such pangs of remorse, especially towards the last of mother's life, when, as I know, she was in a great measure undeceived and feared for the perdition of the souls of her children."

In Mrs. Underhill's book, (written for her by another,) there is an effort to convey the impression that John D. Fox, her father, shared in the belief which she sought to establish in the spiritual origin of the "knockings." Such an implication Mrs. Kane declares to be utterly false. He never manifested in any way a tendency toward such belief; on the contrary, he always showed by his conduct and his manner of speech, the utmost repugnance to it, and a perfect contempt for the weakness which could lead one into it.

Margaret Fox, the mother, used to say to her husband :

"Now, John, don't you see that it's a wonderful thing?"

"No, I don't," he would answer. "Don't talk to me about it. I don't want to hear a word about it!"

Mrs. Margaret Fox Kane says, further: "My father did not believe in Spiritualism. The excitement which we caused annoyed him a great deal. He signed a statement which merely amounted to his declaring that he did not know how the noises originated. He was cajoled into doing this. He wanted to get rid of the importunities of those who believed, or affected to believe, in the 'rappings.'"

Such is the story of the earliest "rappings" at Hydesville.

It is embellished by Mrs. Underhill with many transparent falsehoods. But still further to bolster it up, it was thought necessary to discover traditions, or to invent "hearsay" anecdotes, giving to the house in which they lived a ghostly history. There are few country houses about which the memory of the oldest neighboring inhabitant does not recall something or other remarkable and strange, which was told him by some one or other whose identity is very indefinite, in the dim, distant past. Thus it is stated that odd noises had been heard in the Hydesville house during several previous years by successive occupants. But it is confessed that none of those persons (whose testimony no one pretends to give) had obtained any intelligible messages from another world.

Mrs. Kane states that all of this alleged neighborhood gossip was totally unknown to her at the time, and she believes that it had its chief—or perhaps its only—origin, in the morbid imaginations of those who were the first to set it going.

CHAPTER VIII.

DEVELOPMENT OF THE FRAUD.

Now we come to the moment when Ann Leah Fox Fish, the eldest sister, thirty-one years of age at that time, appears upon the scene of the wondrous and so-called supernatural commotion at the little rustic hamlet of Hydesville.

No "mediumistic" suggestions or impulses had ever come to her. Not one, though she had lived twenty-three years longer in the world than the dark-eyed, fascinating little girl who produced the first mysterious sounds in her mother's home.

The excitement had reached a great height, and a pamphlet was already in the press detailing the whole of the wonderful performances at Hydesville, when Leah first heard of them. She hastened thither at once. Some idea of the profit which could be derived from awakened public interest in the matter, seems to have come to her very promptly. She found that the family had moved from the "haunted" house to that of her brother, David. She investigated the source of the "raps." Mrs. Kane says that one of the first things which she did upon her arrival at the house, was to take both her and Katie apart and to cause them to undress and to show her the manner of producing the mysterious noises. Never for a moment was the cold and calculating brain of the eldest sister a dupe to the cunning pranks of the little children. So interested was she in the matter, that she insisted upon taking back with her to Rochester, at the end of a fortnight, her daughter Lizzie, and Katie, her sister— Maggie not being inclined to go with her. And, in the interval, she practised "rapping" herself, with her toes, after the manner illustrated by the girls. She found great difficulty in producing the same effect, however, as the joints of her feet were no longer as pliable as in childhood. The effort required was also much greater, and never during her whole lifetime did she succeed in attaining to much proficiency in this method of deception. The pronounced movement, necessary in her case to cause even a faint sound to be heard, was easy to detect.

"Often," says Mrs. Kane, "when we were giving séances together, I have been ashamed and mortified by the awkward manner in which she would do it. People would observe the effort she made to produce even moderate 'rappings,' and then they would look at me in suspicion and surprise. It required every bit of my skill and my best tact to prevent them from going away convinced of the imposture."

On the way to Rochester by canal, the "rappings," according to Mrs. Underhill, pursued her. The "Spirits became quite bold and rapped loudly" at the dinner-table in the cabin; "and occasionally" she adds, "*one end of the table would jump up and nearly spill the water out of our glasses; but there was so much noise on the*

DEVELOPMENT OF THE FRAUD.

boat (going through the locks, etc.) that only we, who recognized the sounds, knew of them."

It would be easy, indeed—on this very thin reservation, to the effect that "only we, who recognized the sounds, knew of them"—to denounce the whole of this statement as the grossest falsehood. I have, however, the personal assurance of Mrs. Catharine Fox Jencken that the "rappings" were really heard, but that they were done by her with her feet. On the other hand, she declares that the joggling or lifting of the table never took place; nor did she ever hear of it till Mrs. Underhill's book was published. It may be observed here that the latter carefully refrains from informing us whether the passengers also failed to observe the singular disturbance of the cabin table, at which they were dining.

At Rochester, Mrs. Fish seems to have devoted herself to developing and elaborating the falsehood of Spiritualism. Singularly enough, to this matron, who had never before evinced the least possession of so-called "mediumistic" qualities, all sorts of grotesque and terrorizing wonders now arrived. This is a fair specimen of her narrative, relating to the period in question :

"In the evening, my friend, Jane Little, and two or three other friends, called in to spend an hour or two with us. We sang and I played on the piano; but even then, while the lamp was burning brightly(!), I felt the deep throbbing of the dull accompaniment of the invisibles, keeping time to the music as I played ; but I did not wish to have my visitors know it, and the spirits seemed kind enough not to make themselves heard (!) that others would observe what was so apparent to me."

The book to which I am obliged to refer so constantly, and which is a good example of the bulk of spiritualistic literature, is full of passages ten times as absurd as this one, and having just as strongly the stamp of the crudest and most clumsy invention. For the most part, the only appropriate treatment for such absurdities is contemptuous silence. Occasionally, however, I shall find it necessary, for the sake of completeness in this exposition, to meet them with positive refutation, which in reality they do not deserve.

Having thus got one of the clever and lively little girls under her own control, Leah soon induced her mother to come to Rochester with the other. Nothing could show more clearly that she had already formed the resolve to reap a harvest of gain and renown from this auspicious beginning, than her decisive course, instantly upon realizing the public wonder and curiosity which the "rappings" had excited.

It was absolutely necessary to delude some people who were near, and who should have been dear to her, as well as the careless and easily gullible public. The good and simple-hearted old mother would never have been a partner in conscious deception. The matter-of-fact, unspeculative father, must be brought to a point where he would at least not deny the claims of the so-called "mediums," his daughters. The honest and outspoken Lizzie must be awed into discretion by the prospect of great prosperity, which was opened before them, and the lesson that if she spoke too freely they would surely be deprived of it. Some stalwart and docile sympathizers must be enlisted outside of her own people who could be depended upon to stand by them as against too strenuous inquiry, or hot-tempered public assault.

Immediately upon Margaret's arrival at the house in Rochester, in which Mrs. Fish lived, and which adjoined a graveyard, the "manifestations" redoubled. They were produced by the combined efforts of Leah, Margaret and Katie. Mrs. Underhill narrates that one night, about this time, a "spirit" walked about in their room, as if in his bare feet, when they were all supposed to be in bed. She continues: "He answered my question by stamping on the floor. I was amused—although afraid. He seemed so willing to do my bidding that I could not resist the temptation of speaking to him as he marched around my bed. I said, 'Flat Foot, can you dance the Highland fling?' This seemed to delight him. I sang the music for him, and he danced most admirably. This shocked mother and she said: 'O, Leah, how can you encourage that fiend by singing for him to dance?' I soon found that they took advantage of my familiarity, and gathered in strong force around us. And here language utterly fails to describe the incidents that occurred. Loud whispering, giggling, scuffling, groaning, death-struggles, murder scenes of the most fearful character—I forbear to describe them. Mother became so alarmed that she called to Calvin to come up stairs. He came—angry at the spirits—and declared that 'he would conquer or die in the attempt.' This seemed to amuse them. They went to his bed, raised it up and let it down, and shook it violently. He was still determined not to yield to them.

"Before Calvin came up stairs, and during a short lull in their performances, we quickly removed our beds to the floor, hoping thereby to prevent them from raising us up and letting us down with such violence. Calvin said as he came up, that we were foolish to make our beds on the floor, as it pleased the spirits to see how completely they had conquered us. So he laid down on his bed, and quietly awaited developments. Mother said, 'Calvin, I wish your bed was on the floor, too. We have not been disturbed since we left the bedstead.' Calvin remarked, 'They are up to some deviltry now. I hear them.' He no sooner uttered these words, than a shower of slippers came flying at him as he lay in his bed. He bore this without a murmur. The next instant he was struck violently with his cane. He seized it and struck back, right and left, with all his strength, without hitting anything; but received a palpable *bang* in return for every thrust he made. He sprang to his feet and fought with all his might. Everything thrown at him he pitched back to them, until a brass candlestick was thrown at him, cutting his lip. This quite enraged him. He pronounced a solemn malediction and throwing himself on the bed, he vowed he would have nothing more to do with 'fiendish spirits.'

"He was not long permitted to remain in quiet there. They commenced at his bedstead and deliberately razed it to the floor, leaving the headboard in one place, the footboard in another, the two sides at angles, and the bedclothes scattered about the room. He was left lying on his mattress, and for a moment there was silence; after which some slight movements were heard in the 'green room.' I had stowed a large number of balls of carpet rags in an old chest standing on the floor, with two trunks and several other articles on the top of it. It seemed but the work of a moment for them to get at the carpet balls, which came flying at us in every direction, hitting us in the same place every time. They took us for their target, and threw with the skill of an archer. Darkness made no difference with them, and if either of us attempted to remonstrate against such violence, they would instantly give *the remonstrant* the benefit of a ball."

Mrs. Kane remembers with tolerable distinctness the antics that distinguished this sojourn of her mother, herself and her sisters in the Rochester house. She and Katie did indulge in wild larks in the sleeping rooms of the family at all hours of the night. The "whispering" and "giggling," the "scuffling" and "groaning," and the tragic mimicry were natural to childish daredevils like themselves, and one can well understand how, with the attendant "rappings," the showers of slippers hurled from the "green room," the shaking of Calvin's bed and the "banging" of him on the head, these things may have made the desired impression upon both him and the mother. Mrs. Kane says that this is the true and only explanation of it all, and that in comparatively recent years, at séances in Adelphi Hall, New York, she has done the most audacious things, similar in character to these, under cover of semi-darkness, and has not been detected, simply because nearly all of those who were present were believers and were not too curious,

There is another "evidence" given by Ann Leah which is too pitiably ridiculous to be considered, except as a subject of laughter.

"Often at meal-time," she says, "the table would be gradually agitated, and Calvin in particular, [alas, poor Calvin!] would be more disturbed than the rest of us. Once he arose from his chair and reached across the table for a heavy pitcher of water, when *the chair was instantly removed and he sat down on the floor, spilling the water all over himself!*"

Mrs. Kane's sole comment upon this is: "Of course, we slily did it, as we did many other hoydenish tricks.

"We also used to twitch mother's cap off and gently jerk the comb out of her hair, just to tease her. Leah says that these things were done by the spirits! How silly to address such a puerile pretense to any one gifted with common sense!"

As a companion picture to what has gone before, let the reader also engrave this "miraculous" scene upon the retina of his imagination:

"We had stored our winter provisions in the cellar. Among them were several barrels of apples, potatoes, turnips, etc. From this cellar came the apples, potatoes and turnips flying across our room, hitting all in precisely the same place every time. It will now be remembered that these articles were in the cellar under the ground floor, and had to come from the rear of the cellar, through the door, into the kitchen, up the stairs, into the pantry on the second floor, through the pantry into the dining room, up the second flight of stairs, into the large room in which we slept, hitting us as we lay in our beds near the front window. * * *

"A cabinet shop was the next thing represented by the spirits. They seemed to be possessed of all kinds of tools to work with. After sawing off boards they would let them fall heavily on the floor, jarring everything around them. Then, after planing, jointing, driving nails, and screwing down the lid of a coffin, they would shove the hollow sounding article about the room. (This we understood at a later day.) Often to our utter amazement, pickets from the discarded lots in the cemetery came flying through the room over our heads, on our beds, like debris in a tornado. They came from the extreme west side of the burying-ground, through *that* lot, and the distance of about two hundred feet through *our* lot; an entire distance of about four hundred feet. That they came by no visible means, we knew; as no human power could have thrown them through the air into our chamber window, hitting us in our beds, in the same place every time."

In July, 1848, Leah, her sisters and mother, revisited the Hydesville house, which was then unoccupied. David, the brother, had fallen by this time into the plans of Leah, whether a dupe or an accomplice, Margaret, even at this day, is unable to say. To him was due the very first suggestion that the so-called spirits might communicate with the living by means of the alphabet. And since then, this has been the chief stay of spiritualism, literally the A B C of all its so-called science. It is a singular commentary upon the consistency of the "spirits," or the good faith of those who professed to interpret their messages, that the code of communication at first employed in their circles was entirely different in the meaning of the simple signals used from the one which finally was adopted. Would the "spirits," think you, who are divorced from the trammels of this world, have been guilty of this simple error and have been obliged to correct it afterward, had they not been impostors?

The object of Mrs. Fish in going back to Hydesville is quite apparent. There was yet an unworked mine of wonder and superstition, out of which the dust of dross might be thrown into the eyes of the credulous, as the pure gold of revelation.

In the first place, it was necessary to get from the so-called invisible intelligence an injunction to seek for proofs of the foul murder which it had been said had been committed in the house where the "rappings" were originally heard.

Mind you, months had then elapsed since the digging had been first done in the cellar and the Ganargua creek near by, and David S., who was now wholly in sympathy with Leah in her view of the future importance of the new superstition, had lived in the neighborhood ever since, while nobody had remained in the "haunted" house to be cognizant of what might have taken place there in the mean time.

By the new code system of obtaining answers to queries, a mandate to dig up the cellar and to search for something or other there was obtained, and obeyed, the work lasting two or three days. It is stated by Leah that some fragments of an earthen bowl, a few bones, some teeth and some bunches of hair were found. She says that doctors pronounced the bones to be human.

Of course, the names of these doctors are nowhere to be found in her volume, nor does any one, unwarped by prejudice, really believe more than a very small part of this story.

That there was digging is certain.

That there had been plenty of time to hide anything that David Fox had desired to hide in the cellar, is certain.

Yet Mrs. Kane remembered absolutely nothing about anything having been found in the cellar that bore the slightest semblance to any portion of the human frame. If any bones (perchance, like those found in the creek, the skeleton of a horse) were uncovered, she denies positively that any doctor ever gave the opinion that they were the remains of a man.

She pronounces equally false, the statement of Leah that about the time the digging was abandoned, on account of the angry interference of a mob, the spades of the diggers struck upon a hollow-sounding, wooden substance, which might or might not have been a box of ill-gotten plunder, or the rough sepulchre of the slain pedler.

The indignation of the neighbors of the Foxes in Arcadia was not so much due to the fact that the latter persisted in pretending to communicate with ghosts and uncanny elfs, as it was to the totally unwarranted suspicion which had been cast through the early "rappings" upon a man named Bell, who had formerly lived in the house, which it was now pretended was haunted. This, as well as other evidence of the public feeling at that time, was cleverly employed for her own benefit by Leah, who easily foresaw how anything that might bear the semblance of religious persecution would promote her cause, false though it was, by bringing to it both greater notoriety and widespread sympathy.

There is no doubt, too, that if there had not been a very strong vein of superstition in the Fox family, the first "rappings" would never have produced the deep impression that they did on the mother and her son David. Many strange stories, which had been handed down from a grandfather or a great-grandfather, a great uncle or a great aunt, were told at the fireside with such embellishment as will inevitably come from recital and repetition to a wonder-delighting audience. There were traditions of prophecies fulfilled and of dumb cattle behaving queerly, all of which Mrs. Underhill has very carefully set down and magnified in her own peculiar manner to her own unholy purpose.

CHAPTER IX.

THE MERCENARY CAMPAIGN.

The public campaign of Spiritualism was now begun.

A sufficient hubbub had been made over it to induce attention from all sorts and conditions of people.

The mother and her daughters went again to Rochester, and there placed themselves in the hands of the first of many "committees of friends" who were used as tools or confederates, according to their character, to "humbug" the public more completely. The character and functions of these committees may be judged from the following, which is found in Leah's book: "The names of this committee were Isaac Post, R. D. Jones, Edward Jones. John

Kedzie and Andrew Clackner. *They were faithful friends, who never permitted any one to visit us unattended by themselves or some reliable person.*"

The so-called spirits soon urged in laborious communications that it was needful to make their demonstrations more public, and that an "investigation" of the "rappings," ought therefore to be made by some well-known men. The "spirits" were even so kind as to spell out by means of the tentative alphabet, the names of those whom they wished to have appointed to perform this part. The desire for advertisement, indeed, was not likely to cause the rejection of the name of any available person, whose prominence would increase the public interest in the movement. We are not astonished, then, to find that Frederick Douglass was one of those present at this earliest farce of investigation. It was the forerunner of many others which were like unto it, and gradually, in their stations in various cities, the "Fox Sisters" drew to their séances nearly all

THE MERCENARY CAMPAIGN. 123

of the conspicuous persons of the time, who regarded the effects exhibited to them in as many different lights as their minds and characters were different.

Naturally enough, after this compliance with their desires, the "spirits" directed that a public exhibition should be given. The largest hall in Rochester was hired for the purpose.

And here the infamy of bringing forward two little girls to do the work of base and vulgar charlatanism, appears in all its revolting character. The eldest of the children was then but nine years old. Had she been dressed in accordance with her tender age, it would have taken only very slight observation to detect the secret of the "rappings." Those persons now living, who were present at this and at other public exhibitions of Spiritualism at that time, will easily remember that Margaret and Catherine Fox appeared on a platform in long gowns, as if they had been full-grown women. The dresses were expressly prepared by order of Mrs. Ann Leah

Fox Fish, the evil genius of these unfortunate victims. Without these robes nothing whatever could have been done in the way of "spirit rappings," under the matter-of-fact scrutiny of the public.

To carry out the delusion to the utmost, every detail touching these earliest exhibitions was directed through "spirit rappings," even to the insertion of grandiloquent notices in the newspapers.

In all of the "investigations" of the "rappings," at this or at any other time, the attentive student will find somewhere a loop-hole of escape from observation, an unguarded avenue of detection. In some of the principal séances, described at great length by Leah, the conditions favorable to fraud and illusion were so very obvious that they ought to have excited derision in the veriest child.

The following passage in the report of a so-called investigation, is pointed to by professional spiritualists as one of the best "evidences" of the genuineness of Spiritualism:

"One of the committee placed one of his hands on the feet of the ladies and the other on the floor, and though the feet were not moved, there was a distinct jar of the floor."

Here, then, there were three operators and one investigator. The latter puts his hand on the feet of the ladies. How many feet, pray you? There were six feet on the platform, as we know, all of which had been carefully educated in the production of "raps." Could one man's hand cover them all? And if it could not, does not this pretended "evidence" fall at once to the ground?

All of the recitals made by spiritualistic writers concerning the doings of the "Fox Sisters," contain this element of vagueness, the lack of precision and completeness, which to persons unaccustomed to analysis may possibly appear plausible enough, but to the experienced inquirer is merely a more certain proof of weakness and prevarication.

Volumes might be written to meet the statements advanced in every case, and to show how clumsily misleading they are. It is not worth while at this late day, and in that direction, to do more than I have already accomplished in this chapter.

Indeed, the actual demonstration of the fact that the far-famed "rappings" are produced in the manner described at the beginning of this work, should be quite sufficient to all logical minds, to condemn every claim that the professional mediums have advanced as being the agents of any supernatural manifestations.

The good old Latin maxim never applied with greater force than it does here : *Falsus in unum, falsus in omnibus.*

The operations of the eldest sister all tended to the one end : fame and money. In Rochester, fees for the first time were accepted by "mediums," and shortly afterward a tariff of prices for admission to the séances and the "private circles" was adopted and made public. No jugglers ever drove a more prosperous business than did the "Fox family" for a number of years, when once fairly launched upon that sea of popular wonder, which somebody has said is supplied by the inherent fondness of mankind for being humbugged.

Mrs. Fish had actually the project of founding a new religion, and she tried hard to convince her younger sisters and her own child that there were really such things as spiritual communications, notwithstanding that all of those that were produced in their séances they knew to be perfectly false. She asserted that even before Maggie and Katie were born she had received messages warning her that they were destined to do great things.

"In all of our séances, while we were under her charge," says Mrs. Kane, "we knew just when to rap 'yes' and when to rap 'no' by signals that she gave us, and which were unknown to any one but ourselves. Of course, we were too young, then, to have been successful very long in deluding people, had it not been for an arrangement such as this,

"Her own daughter, Lizzie, had no manner of patience with her transparent pretence.

"'Ma,' she would exclaim, when Leah attempted to impress her with a belief in some of the frauds which she perpetrated, 'how can you ever pretend that that is done by the spirits? I am ashamed to know even that you do such things—it's dreadfully wicked.'"

Some day it will be known that one other person beside Lizzie, who afterwards occupied a filial relation to this woman, detested even more strongly the atmosphere of hypocrisy and deceit with which the latter surrounded herself, and hated, too, the rankling obligation under which an unkind fate had placed her.

It is not so wonderful that men of learning and originality were drawn to the mysterious séances of the Fox girls, when it is considered that they became a sort of fashionable "fad," as the receptions of Mesmer did in the last century in Paris. There were great opportunities there for studying human nature, and the period was one of a notable awakening of scientific and transcendental speculation. Such men as Greeley, Bancroft, Fenimore Cooper, Bryant, N. P. Willis, Dr. Francis, John Bigelow, Ripley, Dr. Griswold, Dr. Eliphalet Nott, Theodore Parker, William M. Thackeray, James Freeman Clarke, Thomas M. Foote and Bayard Taylor, and women of the intellectual strength of Alice Cary and Harriet Beecher Stowe became deeply interested. But nearly all of these lost their interest in Spiritualism in time, for they became morally, if not positively convinced, that the effects produced were the mere result of fraud.

There was another attraction, however, in those early days. The younger "mediums" were both very pretty and very young. Sympathy and commiseration, as much as aught else, often drew visitors to them, and caused such visitors to continue their friends. Thus, we find that Horace Greeley and Dr. Elisha Kent Kane became important factors in the lives of both of these interesting creatures, the former educating Katie, and the latter striving to form Maggie's mind and to reform her character with the express object of making her his wife.

Mrs. Kane, in commenting upon the life which she led at that time, says:

"When I look back, I can only say in defense of my depraved calling, that I took not the slightest pleasure in it. The novelty and the excitement that had half intoxicated me as a child were fast being dissipated. The true conception of this infamous thing soon dawned upon me. The awakening was full of anguish—the anguish of hope, as well as the anguish of grief. I then first knew Dr. Kane, and with that acquaintance entered the new light into my life."

CHAPTER X.

SPIRITUALISTIC BOOMERANGS.

In nearly all of the so-called investigations of the "rappings" produced by the "Fox Sisters," there was an absolute absence of genuine scientific inquiry. Only once in this critical stage of their career, did they submit to experiment and examination by doctors of unquestioned repute and learning. The result of this investigation has been held up by professional spiritualists as a triumphant proof that the source of "rappings" was beyond any mortal finding out. The fact is that the doctors hit upon the right principle at the inception of the inquiry, but were misled into a wrong application of it, an error which the "mediums," of course, encouraged up to a certain point, so that they might gain prestige afterwards by refuting it. Following out this policy,

Mrs. Underhill has incorporated in her book the testimony of the doctors, heedless of the law of destiny, that truth must prevail finally.

I propose to take this same statement of the doctors, based as it is upon an erroneous assumption and a correct theory, and show how strongly it sustains and plainly corroborates the explanation of the "rappings" now given by Mrs. Kane and Mrs. Jencken.

The gentlemen who made this notable investigation are usually spoken of as the "Buffalo doctors." They were members of the faculty of the University of Buffalo. Austin Flint, who afterward held the highest medical rank in the metropolis, was the most prominent of the three. The other two were Drs. Charles A. Lee and C. B. Coventry.

The theory that they advanced was that the mysterious noises were produced by some one of the articulations of the body. Their assumption was that it was the great joint of the knee which produced them. Had they worked upon their theory alone, and left all assumption aside, until actual evidence had led up to them ; or, even had they investigated other joints of the lower limbs, besides that of the knee, they must have inevitably arrived at the correct conclusion. Unfortunately, however, the idea which so beset them as to render their labor abortive, arose from the actual existence in Buffalo of a woman whose knee-joints could be snapped audibly at will.

The closeness of the scrutiny applied by these gentlemen displeased the eldest "medium," and her resentment finds characteristic expression in her volume, printed thirty-seven years after the occurrence. She declares that she found Dr. Lee to be "a wily, deceitful man."

If anything can circumvent cunning, it is certainly cunning itself, and in this sense, it is entirely laudable when exerted in a proper cause. There is no doubt that strategy had to be used to induce this woman, conscious of her falsity, and schooled in subterfuges and evasions, to submit to a coldly scientific test. The challenge, however, came under such circumstances, public suspicion being so whetted by the fact that a woman had been discovered whose knee-joints possessed the peculiar quality of making sound, that it could not well be avoided, without it becoming generally known that the declination was a tacit confession of fraud.

The doctors published very promptly the result of their preliminary examination, which was made without any special facilities being afforded them.

They said:

"Curiosity having led us to visit the rooms at the Phelps House, in which two females from Rochester, Mrs. Fish and Miss Fox, profess to exhibit striking manifestations from the spirit world, by means of which communion may be had with deceased friends, etc.; and having arrived at a physiological explanation of the phenomena, the correctness of which has been demonstrated in an instance which has since fallen under our observation, we have felt that a public statement is called for, which may, perhaps, serve to prevent a further waste of time, money and credulity (to say nothing of sentiment and philosophy) in connection with this so long successful imposition.

"The explanation is reached almost by a logical necessity, on the application of a method of reasoning much resorted to in the diagnosis of diseases, namely, *the reasoning by exclusion*.

"It was reached by this method prior to the demonstration which has subsequently occurred.

"It is to be assumed, first, that the manifestations are not to be regarded as spiritual, provided they can be physically or physiologically accounted for. Immaterial agencies are not to be invoked until material agencies fail. We are thus to *exclude* spiritual causation in this stage of the investigation.

"Next, it is taken for granted that the 'rappings' are not produced by artificial contrivances about the persons of the females, which may be concealed by the dress. This hypothesis is excluded because it is understood that the females have been repeatedly and carefully examined by lady committees.

"It is obvious that the 'rappings' are not caused by machinery attached to tables, doors, etc., for they are heard in different rooms, and in different parts of the same room in which the females are present, *but always near the spot where the females are stationed.* This mechanical hypothesis is then to be excluded. So much for the negative evidence, and now for what positively relates to the subject.

"*On carefully observing the countenances of the two females it is evident that they involve an effort of the will. They evidently attempted to conceal any indications of voluntary effort, but did not succeed. A voluntary effort was manifested, and it was plain that it could not be continued very long without fatigue.* Assuming, then, this *positive fact*, the inquiry arises, how can the will be exerted to produce sounds ('rappings') without obvious movements of the body?

The voluntary muscles themselves are the only organs, save those which belong to the mind itself, over which volition can exercise any direct control. But contractions of the muscles do not, in the muscles themselves, occasion obvious sounds. The muscles, therefore, to develop audible vibrations, must act upon parts with which they are connected. Now, it was sufficiently clear that the 'rappings' were not *vocal* sounds ; these could not be produced without movements of the respiratory muscles, which would at once lead to detection. Hence, excluding vocal sounds, *the only possible source of the noises in question, produced as we have seen that they must be, by voluntary muscular contraction, is in one or more of the movable articulations of the skeleton*, from the anatomical construction of the voluntary muscles. This explanation remains as *the only alternative.*

"By an analysis prosecuted in this manner we arrive at the conviction that the 'rappings,' assuming that they are not spiritual, *are produced by the action of the will, through voluntary action on the joints.*

"Various facts may be cited to show that the motion of the joints, under certain circumstances, is adequate to produce the phenomena of the 'rappings.' * * * By a curious coincidence, after arriving at the above conclusion respecting the source of the sounds, *an instance has fallen under our observation, which demonstrates the fact that noises precisely identical with the spiritual 'rappings' may be produced in the knee-joints.*"

The doctors then describe how the sounds may be produced in certain subjects by the partial dislocation of the knee joint; and they add:

"The visible vibrations of articles in the room, situated near the operator, occur if the limb, or any portion of the body, is *in contact with them* at the time the sounds are produced. *The force of the semi-dislocation of the bone is sufficient to occasion distinct jarring of the doors, tables, etc., if in contact.* The intensity of the sound may be varied in proportion to the force of the muscular contractions, and this will render the apparent source of the 'rappings' more or less distinct."

I have italicized the portions of these extracts which apply in a measure to the action of the toe-joints, as well as to that of the knee. No especial comment upon them is needed. The reader may easily comprehend the relation of these peculiar facts.

Knowing, from this brief of their supposed case, exactly what she had to apprehend from them, and anxious to prove triumphantly that she and her sisters did not make the "rappings" with their knees, Mrs. Fish rushed into print, and challenged the doctors to a more public investigation, to be made by three men and three women, the latter of whom were to disrobe the "mediums," if they so desired. The doctors, of course, accepted.

In her account of this scene, Mrs. Fish speaks of herself and her sister Maggie as "two young creatures thus baited as it were by cruel enemies." It should be remembered at this point that her age at that time was about thirty-four years, whilst that of Maggie was only eleven! So much for the disingenuousness of the narrator.

She herself says that during the test, Maggie and she sat on a sofa together a long time and no raps came. The watch was too close. Then a zealous and indiscreet friend rapped on the back of her chair, and to shield herself from seeming complicity, she rebuked him with great ostentation. How kindly she felt toward fraud, however, is shown by the excuses which she makes for his conduct.

"It was certainly a severe and cruel ordeal for us," she goes on, "as we sat there under that accusation, surrounded by all these men, authorities, some of them persecutors, *while the raps, usually so ready and familiar, would not come to our relief. Some few and faint ones did indeed come—some nine or ten. The doctors say in their account that it was while they intermitted the holding of our feet.* Such was not my *impression,* but *I* attach *small importance* to that."

There were several sittings of the investigators in company with the "mediums," and Mrs. Underhill asserts that at times plentiful "rappings" were heard, both when their feet and knees were held and when they were not held. And then she introduces this weak and transparent piece of hypocrisy so familiar to those who have ever had to do with so-called "mediums":

"We are now familiar with the fact that spirits often refuse to act in the presence of those who bring to the occasion, not a candid and fair spirit of inquiry for the satisfaction of an honest skepticism, but a bitter and offensive bigotry of prejudice and invincible hostility, which does not really seek, but rather repels the truth, and but little deserves the favor of its exhibition to them by the spirits."

The further report of the doctors contained these points:

"*The two females were seated upon two chairs placed near together, their heels resting on cushions, their lower limbs extended, with the toes elevated and the feet separated from each other. The object of this experiment was to secure a position in which the ligaments of the knee-joint* should be made tense, and no opportunity offered to make a pressure with the foot. *We were pretty well satisfied that the displacement of the bones requisite for the sounds could not be effected, unless a fulcrum were obtained by resting one foot upon the other, or on some resisting body. The company waited half an hour, but no sounds were heard in this position.*

"The position of the *younger* sister was then changed to a sitting posture, with the lower limbs extended on the sofa, *the elder sister sitting in the customary way*, at the other extremity of the sofa. The 'Spirits' did not choose to signify their presence under these circumstances, although repeatedly requested to do so. The latter experiment went to confirm the belief that the *younger sister alone* produced the 'rappings.' These experiments were continued until the females themselves admitted that it was useless to continue any longer at that time, with any expectation of manifestations being made.

"*In resuming the usual position on the sofa,*

the feet resting on the floor, the knockings soon began to be heard."

Then the doctors held the knees of the fair performers to ascertain if there was any movement when the sounds were heard:

"The hands were kept in apposition for several minutes at a time, and the experiments repeated frequently, for the space of half an hour and more, with negative results; that is to say, *there were plenty of 'raps' when the knees were not held, and none when the hands were applied, save once; as the pressure was intentionally relaxed (Dr. Lee being the holder) two or three faint single 'raps' were heard, and Dr. Lee immediately averred that the motion of the bone was plainly perceptible to him. The experiment of siezing the knees as quickly as possible, when the knockings first commenced, was tried several times, but always with the effect of putting an immediate quietus upon the demonstrations."*

No sensible person can doubt that the statements of facts within their actual knowledge, made by these three eminent physicians, are absolutely true. They say finally:

"*Had our experiments, which were first directed to this joint failed, we should have proceeded to interrogate, experimentally, other articulations. But the conclusions seemed clear that the 'Rochester knockings' emanate from the knee-joint.*"

What a pity they did *not* "interrogate" other articulations!

The report, erroneous as it was in its conclusions, contained so much significant truth that Mrs. Fish was at first staggered by its purport. But in March, 1851, she wrote again to the press a lengthy letter, in which she feebly attempted to counteract the effect of the doctor's opinion, and incidentally made some grave admissions. Referring to the fact that whenever the "mediums" were kept in constrained positions there were no "manifestations," she made this remarkable admission:

"*It is true that when our feet were placed on*

cushions stuffed with shavings, and resting on our heels, there were no sounds heard, and that sounds were heard when our feet were resting on the floor; and it is just as true that if our friendly spirits retired when they witnessed such harsh proceedings on the part of our persecutors, it was not in our power to detain them."

Then she remarks that certain things happened *after the medical gentlemen left:*

"Our feet were held from the floor by Dr. Gray and Mr. Clark, in presence of the whole committee, on the evening of the investigation made by the medical gentlemen (after they left); and the sounds were distinctly heard, which was allowed by the committee to be a far more satisfactory test, as they could distinctly hear the sounds under the feet, and feel the floor *jar* while our feet were held nearly or quite a foot from the floor."

About this time, a suspicion that the "raps" were made by use of the toes, first found expression, but it never seems to have been followed up to the point of verification. Indeed, the secret seems to have been kept absolutely for forty years, and was only revealed by the lips of Mrs. Margaret Fox Kane.

I cannot refrain from quoting in this place an incident from the record of the common enemy, which further illustrates the imbecile audacity with which they parade their abominable fraud before the eyes of sensible persons. At a séance, in which wonderous things were done under a table, around which the company including Mrs. Fish and one of her sisters were closely seated, one, Mr. Stringham, apparently a doubter, asked:

"May I leave the table while the others remain, that I may look and see the bells ringing?"

The "spirits" answered:

"What do you think we require you to sit close to the table for?"

And the veracious writer adds:

"*When spirits make these physical demonstra-*

tions, they are compelled to assume shapes that human eyes must not look upon."

! ! ! ! ! ! ! ! !

I should be guilty of an historical omission did I not also notice a somewhat formal investigation made by a committee of Harvard Professors and others, appointed to satisfy the exigencies of a newspaper controversy in Boston in 1857, and which Mrs. Ann Leah Fox Brown and Miss Catherine Fox attended. The results were wholly unsatisfactory and inconclusive from a scientific standpoint, though the moral effect of this outcome was strongly against the spiritualists, who were, of course, bound to prove their positive side of the case, and failed ignominiously to do so. The committee consisted of Professors Agassiz, Pierce and Horsford, Mr. George Lunt, editor of the Boston *Courier*, Dr. A. B. Gould, Mr. Allen Putnam, Dr. H. F. Gardner and Mr. G. W. Rains. The last three were pronounced spiritualists.

Professor Agassiz, who in particular had

studied mesmerism and so-called clairvoyance most carefully, and who believed to some extent in the former, declared with emphasis that there was an easy physiological explanation of all the effects that the "Fox Sisters," or any other "rappers," produced. The raps caused by the "Fox Sisters" on this occasion were but feeble and uncertain. When other "mediums" were under examination, the close watch kept upon them by the learned investigators seemed greatly to disconcert them and prevented the possibility of any pronounced "manifestations" taking place.

The *Courier* had issued a challenge offering five hundred dollars to any one who would "communicate a single word imparted to the 'spirits,'" by its editor "in an adjoining room," who would "read a single word in English, written inside a book or sheet of paper folded in such a manner as we may suggest; who would answer with the aid of all the higher intelligences he or she can invoke from the other world, *three questions* * * *;" and it added:

"And we will not require Dr. Gardiner or the 'mediums' to risk a single cent on the experiment. If one or all of them can do one of these things, the five hundred dollars shall be paid on the spot. If they fail, they shall pay nothing; not even the expense incident to trying the experiment."

The Committee made a report which declared that nothing had been done which entitled any one to receive the sum offered by the *Courier*. Therefore no award was made.

A library might be written containing only accounts of private investigations of "spiritual phenomena" by able and scientific observers, all of which conduced to but one verdict, that every pretense of Spiritualism is a fraud. I deem it more appropriate, however, and entirely adequate to my purpose, to restrict my citations from such inquiries to those which had an absolutely undeniable official or authoritative character.

CHAPTER XI.

THE SUPREME AUDACITY OF FRAUD.

The multitude of forms that a certain kind of deception, when once it obtains a foothold in the public mind, will assume, is often wonderful.

Spiritualism has resorted to all the trickery that for ages has been used to delude and delight the populace.

Much of it could be traced back to the very first mountebanks who wandered about the streets of the ancient cities, or squatted at the gates of palaces or in market-places to catch the frequent obolus from the curious passer-by.

In every country under the sun, the trade of deception has been turned to the account of religious superstition. The Hindus, in particular, excel in this branch of necromancy. The marvelous things that Aaron and the Egyptian sorcerers did before Pharaoh, are really as nothing compared with what the modern jugglers of India and China perform. All of the developments of the art that have taken place in the West, seem but trivial imitation beside these, and indeed they are little better.

No sooner had Spiritualism made many proselytes, than there was no limit to its audacious pretensions. Its apostles imagined that they could go on duping the world and even hoodwinking the scientists, and that by appealing to the Federal government for a formal investigation of its claims, which they could not have believed for a moment would be granted, they could obtain a sort of quasi-official recognition of their so-called new religion.

Accordingly, on the 17th of April, 1854, a petition was sent to Congress, bearing fifteen thousand names, and was presented in executive session by Senator Shields of Illinois. As a rather skillful contemporaneous characterization of the matter, what he said on this occasion is of historical interest. The following were his words:

I beg leave to present to the Senate a petition, with some fifteen thousand names appended to it, upon a very singular and novel subject. The petitioners declare that certain physical and mental phenomena of mysterious import, have become so prevalent in this country and Europe, as to engross a large share of public attention. A partial analysis of these phenomena attest the existence, first, of an occult force which is exhibited in sliding, raising, arresting, holding, suspending, and otherwise disturbing ponderable bodies, apparently in direct opposition to the acknowledged laws of matter, and transcending the accredited power of the human mind. Secondly, lights of different degrees of intensity appear in dark rooms, where chemical action or phosphorescent illumination cannot be developed, and where there are no means of generating electricity, or of producing combustion. Thirdly, a variety of sounds, frequent in occurrence, and diversified in character, and of singular significance and importance, consisting of mysterious rapping, indicating the presence of invisible intelligence. Sounds are often heard like those produced by the prosecution of mechanical operations, like the hoarse murmur of the winds and waves, mingled with the harsh creaking of the masts and rigging of a ship laboring in a sea. Concussions also occur, resembling distant thunder, producing oscillatory movements of surrounding objects, and a tremulous motion of the premises upon which these phenomena occur. Harmonious sounds, as those of human voices, and other sounds resembling those of the fife, drum, trumpet, etc., have been produced without any visible agency. Fourthly, all the functions of the human body and mind are influenced in what appear to be certain abnormal states of the system, by causes not yet adequately understood or accounted for. The occult force, or invisible power, frequently interrupts the normal operations of the faculties, suspending sensation and voluntary motion of the body to a death-like coldness and rigidity, and diseases hitherto considered incurable, have been entirely eradicated by this mysterious agency. The petitioners proceed to state that two opinions prevail with respect to the origin of these phenomena. One ascribes them to the power and intelligence of departed spirits operating upon the elements which pervade all natural forms. The other rejects this conclusion, and contends that all these results may be accounted for in a rational and satisfactory manner.

The memorialists, while thus disagreeing as to the cause, concur in the opinion as to the occurrence of the alleged phenomena; and in view of their origin, nature and bearing upon the interests of mankind, demand for them a patient, rigid, scientific investigation, and request the appointment of a scientific commission for that purpose.

I have now given a faithful synopsis of this petition, which, however unprecedented in itself, has been prepared with singular ability, presenting the subject with great delicacy and moderation. I make it a rule to present any petition to the Senate, which is respectful in its terms; but having discharged this duty, I may be permitted to say that the prevalence of this delusion at this age of the world, among any considerable portion of our citizens, must originate, in my opinion, in a defective system of education, or in a partial derangement of the mental faculties, produced by a diseased condition of the physical organization. I cannot, therefore, believe that it prevails to the extent indicated in this petition.

Different ages of the world have had their peculiar delusions. Alchemy occupied the attention of eminent men for several centuries; but there was something sublime in alchemy. The philosopher's stone, or the transmutation of base metals into gold, the *elixir vitæ*, or 'water of life,' which would preserve youth and beauty, and prevent old age, decay and death, were blessings which poor humanity ardently desired, and which alchemy sought to discover by perseverance and piety, Roger Bacon, one of the greatests alchemists and greatest men of the thirteenth century, while searching for the philosopher's stone, discovered the telescope, burning glasses, and gunpowder. The prosecution of that delusion led, therefore, to a number of useful discoveries. In the sixteenth century flourished Cornelius Agrippa, alchemist, astrologer, and magician, one of the greatest professors of hermetic philosophy that ever lived. He had all the spirits of the air and demons of the earth under his command. Paulus Jovious says that the devil, in the shape of a large black dog, attended Agrippa wherever he went. Thomas Nash says, at the request of Lord Surrey, Erasmus, and other learned men, Agrippa called up from the grave several of the great philosophers of antiquity, among others, Sully, whom he caused to deliver his celebrated oration for Roscius, to please the emperor, Charles IV. He summoned David and King Solomon from the tomb, and the Emperor conversed with them long upon the science of government. This was a glorious exhibition of spiritual power, compared with the insignificant manifestations of the present day. I will pass over the celebrated Paracelsus, for the purpose of making allusion to an Englishman, with whose veracious history every one ought to make himself acquainted. In the sixteenth century, Dr. Dee made such progress in the talismanic mysteries, that he acquired ample power to hold familiar conversation with spirits and angels, and to learn from them all the secrets of the universe. On the occasion, the angel Uriel gave him a black crystal of a convex form, which he had only to gaze upon intently, and by a strange effort of the will, he could summon any spirit he wished, to reveal to him the secrets of futurity. Dee, in his veracious diary, says that one day while he was sitting with Alburtus Laski, a Polish nobleman, there seemed to come out of the oratory a spiritual creature, like a pretty girl of seven or nine years of age, with her hair rolled up before and hanging down behind, with a gown of silk, of changeable red and green, and with a train. She seemed to play up and down, and to go in and out behind the books, and as she seemed to get between them, the books displaced themselves and made way for her. This I call a spiritual manifestation of the most interesting and fascinating kind. Even the books felt the fascinating influence of this spiritual creature; for they displaced themselves and made way for her. Edward Kelly, an Irishman, who was present, and who witnessed this beautiful apparition, verifies the doctor's statement; therefore it would be unreasonable to doubt a story so well attested, particularly when the witness was an Irishman. Dr. D. was the distinguished favorite of kings and queens, a proof that spiritual science was in high repute in the good old age of Queen Elizabeth. But of all the professors of occult science, hermetic philosophy or Spiritualism, the Rosicrucians were the most exalted and refined. With them the possession of the philosopher's stone was to be the means of health and happiness, an instrument by which man could command the services of superior beings, control the elements, defy the abstractions of time and space, and acquire the most intimate knowledge of all the secrets of the universe. These were objects worth struggling for. The refined Rosicrucians were utterly disgusted with the coarse, gross, sensual spirits who had been in communication with man previous to their day; so they decreed the annihilation of them all, and substituted in their stead, a race of mild, beautiful and beneficent beings.

The "spirits" of the olden time were a malignant race, and took especial delight in doing mischief; but the new generation is mild and benignant. These "spirits," as this petition attests, indulge in the most innocent amusements and harmless recreations, such as sliding, raising and tipping tables, producing pleasing sounds and variegated sights, and sometimes curing diseases which were previously considered incurable; and for the existence of this simple and benignant race our petitioners are indebted to the brethren of the rosy cross. Among the modern professors of Spiritualism,

Cagliostro was the most justly celebrated. In Paris, his saloons were thronged with the rich and noble. To old ladies he sold immortality, and to the young ones he sold beauty that would endure for centuries, and his charming countess gained immense wealth, by granting attendant sylphs to such ladies as were rich enough to pay for their services. The "Biographies des Contemporains," a work which our present mediums ought to consult with care, says there was hardly a fine lady in Paris who would not sup with the shade of Lucretius in the apartments of Cagliostro. There was not a military officer who would not discuss the art with Alexander, Hannibal or Cæsar, or an advocate or counselor who would not argue legal points with the ghost of Cicero. These were spiritual manifestations worth paying for, and all our degenerate "mediums" would have to hide their diminished heads in the presence of Cagliostro.

It would be a curious inquiry to follow this occult science through all its phases of mineral magnetism, animal mesmerism, etc., until we reach the present, latest and slowest phase of all spiritual manifestation; but I have said enough to show the truth of Burk's beautiful aphorism, "The credulity of dupes is as inexhaustible as the invention of knaves."

A writer of that time says:

"A pleasant debate followed. Mr. Petit proposed to refer the petition of the Spiritualists to three thousand clergymen. Mr. Weller proposed to refer it to the Committee on Foreign Relations, as it might be necessary to inquire whether or not when Americans leave this world they lose their citizenship. Mr. Mason proposed that it should be left to the Committee on Military affairs. General Shields himself said he had thought of proposing to refer the petition to the Committee on Post Offices and Post Roads, because there may be a possibility of establishing a spiritual telegraph between the material and spiritual worlds. The petition was finally, by a decisive vote, laid upon the table. The table did not, as we learn, tip in indignation at this summary disposal of Spiritualism in the Senate, by which we must infer that the 'spirits,' if there were any in the Senate at that time, endorsed its action and considered the same all right."

I might here enter into a description of the various forms of modern spiritualistic representations. It would be a waste of time. I wish, however, to allude more particularly just here to one of the "evidences" which Mrs. Ann Leah Underhill apparently values most highly in connection with the claim of inherent and herditary "mediumistic" powers residing in certain individuals and families. This is the somewhat noted so-called exhibition of "mediumistic" ability by a child of Mrs. Kate Fox Jencken, a babe, only about six weeks old at the time that it began. It is needless to go into all the details of the wonders attributed to little "Ferdie" Jencken, now a fine lad of fifteen, which rest wholly upon the testimony of persons who were interested in magnifying them to the greatest extent. Shadowy forms are said to have appeared to his nurse while she was watching him. At three months he was said to have articulated "Mamma!" But the cap of the climax is the feat he is said to have performed when not six months old. As he was restless one day, his mother gave him a piece of blotting paper and a pencil to play with. He made some marks on the paper and dropped it. When his mother picked it up she exclaimed to Mrs. Underhill, the only other person present:

"See here, he was written something."

It is pretended that on one side of the blotting paper was the message:

"Grandma is here.
"BOYSIE."

Later and up to the close of his first year, he was said to write other messages, but all under like circumstances.

Mrs. Underhill lays great stress upon these "manifestations" in two portions of her work.

The simple and only comment to be made upon them is, that Mrs. Catherine Fox Jencken now declares that they were fraudulent. The messages were in every case written upon the paper before it was placed in the baby's hands, the mother knowing, of course, that a child a few months old would not retain anything very long in its grasp, that those who chanced to be present would not observe, unless previously warned, whether it was wholly blank or not, and that the picking up of the paper from the floor would give ample opportunity to turn undermost the side on which the child may have really scratched some unmeaning marks.

So much for that and kindred marvels of infant "mediumship."

"Ferdie" Jencken, so far as is known, has never, since that early period of his existence, exhibited any "mediumistic power."

The character of the communications purporting to come from the "spirit-land" has always been such as to condemn them, even if nothing else would, in the mind of any one gifted with a clear judgment. How many have read with a bitter sneer those pretended words from "the great ones of the earth," which would place them, if they had really written or uttered them in the unseen life, on a mere level with the emptiest-headed mortals whom we know in this!

"Alas!" exclaims Nathaniel Hawthorne in "The Blythedale Romance," "methinks we have fallen on an evil age! If these phenomena have not humbug at the bottom, so much the worse for us. What can they indicate in a spiritual way, except that the soul of man is descending to a lower point that it has ever reached while incarnate? We are pursuing a downward course in the eternal march, and thus bring ourselves into the same range with beings whom death—in requital of their gross and evil lives—has degraded below humanity. To hold intercourse with spirits of this order, we must stoop and grovel in some elements more vile than earthly dust. These goblins, if they exist at all, are but the shadows of past mortality—mere refuse stuff, adjudged unworthy of the eternal world, and as the most favorable supposition, dwindling gradually into nothingness. The less we have to say to them, the better, lest we share their fate."

CHAPTER XII.

A SCIENTIFIC JURY.

At one period of her strange career, Mrs. Kane entered the service of Mr. Henry Seybert, the famous and wealthy spiritualist of Philadelphia, who proposed to found what he called a "Spiritual Mansion."

Mrs. Kane's salary and appointments were liberal, and her situation was one which would have met the fondest wishes of many noted and ambitious "mediums." She was the high priestess of this new temple of the unseen entities, and as such she was honored and treated with most exalted respect.

The conditions of the "Spiritual Mansion" were in all respects favorable to the intercourse of dwellers in the flesh with those who inhabit the realm of shadows, if such there had been.

The taking up of her abode in this singular institution was one of her earliest steps, after the throwing off of her deep weeds of mourning, worn in memory of the untimely termination of her dream of happiness. It was then that she found that the professional life of a "medium" was the only refuge left her from the cruel pursuit of poverty and want.

But her stay in the "Spiritual Mansion" was short. She had thought that the quiet existence afforded her there would be preferable to the daily and distasteful practice of public "mediumship," which she must have resorted to at once, had she not accepted the proposition of Mr. Seybert. But the hypocrisy unconsciously required of her by him, while of a more fantastic description, was altogether too much for her to endure. Her intense hatred of her profession as a "medium" appeared in a strong light to those who were then in her confidence.

Mrs. Kane, at the "Spiritual Mansion," not only produced pretended messages from the departed friends of her patron, but also from nearly every martyr and saint in the Protestant calendar, and from the famous sages and rulers of old. But her imposture stopped short of actual sacrilege. Beyond that line she never has gone.

When it came to transmitting messages demanded by the living of the apostles and fathers of the church, she revolted against this mania for the supernatural and the impossible, and she refused to continue longer the instrument of pure religious insanity.

She declined to produce "spirit rappings," as emanating from St. Paul, St. Peter, Elijah and the angel Gabriel.

It has often been said that Henry Seybert had an undoubted vein of madness in his brain. Mrs. Kane herself so declares. I believe the same is true of every person (not a knave at heart) who persistently, after reason and conscientious research have demonstrated the truth of the charges against Spiritualism, still refuses to be convinced.

There was, however, a method in the madness of Seybert. Mrs. Kane has always been most careful not to make any positive asseveration of the claims of Spiritualism. Her guarded and, in some measure, candid course, no doubt tended very far towards influencing him to desire an honest and thorough investigation of the so-called spiritualistic phenomena, to be conducted according to the most rigid scientific methods. In his will, he left provision for the founding of a chair of philosophy in the University of Pennsylvania, with the careful stipulation that a certain portion of the income to be derived from the foundation should be devoted to the investigation of "all systems of morals, religion or philosophy which assume to represent the truth; and particularly of modern Spiritualism."

Thus this legacy gave birth to the celebrated "Seybert Commission," whose labors have resulted in the most valuable exposé, prior to this present publication, of the fraudulent methods of Spiritualism—"the tricks of the trade," as it were —which has ever been made.

Even the investigation of the remarkable "rappings," produced by Mrs. Kane, in which the Commission engaged—while less successful than any other branch of their researches—went so far as fully to convince them that these alleged manifestations were entirely fraudulent, and that they were produced by physical action on the part of the "medium," probably by or in the vicinity of her feet.

This they were unable to prove, however, by any use of their five senses, which they were permitted to make. Mrs. Kane gave them no such chance of examination, on this occasion, as had been vouchsafed to the Buffalo doctors some thirty-six years before, almost with the result of throttling Spiritualism in its infancy. No; she was much too clever for that. She would greatly have preferred, to being ignominiously found out, to make a public and unreserved confession.

The fact is that no other scientific committee ever enjoyed the facilities of close observation of the production of the "raps" which were accorded to the "Buffalo doctors," and that, up to this final day, when Mrs. Kane herself tells the truth, there has been not one single positive exposure of the primitive fraud of the "toe-knockings." Conjectures, it is true, have groped in that direction, time and again—but they never have done more than to grope.

The members of the "Seybert Commission" were extremely eager to obtain sittings with Mrs. Kane, and were successful at an early stage of their studies in doing so. Mr. Horace Howard Furness of Philadelphia was acting chairman of the Commission a good part of the time, and as such he wrote to Mrs. Kane in the following very urgent manner:

"222 WEST WASHINGTON SQUARE.
"DEAR MRS. KANE:
"I wrote to you some ten days ago, but, since I have not heard from you, fear that my letter has miscarried, and will therefore repeat it.

"I am anxious, very anxious, that the 'Seybert Commission,' of which I am the chairman, should have an opportunity of investigating the 'Rappings.' Will you, therefore, appoint some day and hour, at your earliest convenience, when I can visit you in New York and make arrangements with you personally?

"I sincerely trust that your summer has been healthful and peaceful, and beg to subscribe myself
"Yours respectfully,
"HORACE HOWARD FURNESS.
"22nd October, 1884."

Mrs. Kane became the guest of Mr. Furness at his house, and there produced the "rappings" at two seances, which were full of important significance.

The first was on the 5th of November, 1884, in the evening. The company consisted of Dr. William Pepper and his wife, Dr. Joseph Leidy, Dr. George A. Koeing, Prof. Robert Ellis Thompson, Mr. Horace Howard Furness, Mr. George S. Fullerton, Mr. Coleman Sellers, all, excepting the lady, members of the Commission, and Mr. George S. Pepper, Miss Logan, and the "medium."

All seated themselves around an open dining-table, Mrs. Kane at one end and Mr. Sellers at the other. The report of the Commission says :

"The medium sat with her feet partly under the table, and consequently concealed from most of those present—her feet were hidden also by her dress."

After the usual preliminaries of an introduction to denizens of the "spirit land," the soul of Henry Seybert was announced. He declared through the "medium" that he knew the names of the members of the Commission, and particularly of the one who was addressing him. Mr. Sellers, who happened to be this person, requested the spirit to spell his name by the aid of a written alphabet, each letter of which was pointed to in turn, the letter intended by the "spirit" being indicated by three "raps." The result was that the name spelled out was the following :

"CHARLES CERI !"

Without commenting upon this blunder of the

"spirit," the Commission encouraged Mrs. Kane to proceed. She took a station at some distance from the table, her hands resting upon the back of a chair, and "raps" were heard which seemed to come from a point very near or under her. Again, when she stood close to a bookcase, "raps" were produced which she declared to proceed from the glass door upon which Mr. Sellers rested his hand. The latter felt not the slightest vibration of the glass. Mrs. Kane then produced written messages, addressed to two persons present, whose names she might have ascertained with very great ease. The writing was an irregular scrawl, running from the left, and leaning backward, and could only be read from the observe side by holding the paper up to the light.

The second séance in which Mrs. Kane acted as "medium" took place at the same place on the 6th of November, 1884. Dr. Leidy, Mr. Furness, Dr. Koeing, Mr. Fullerton and Mr. Sellers, members of the Commission, Mr. George S. Pepper, Mrs. Kane and a stenographer were present. The experiments of this evening were more lengthy and exhaustive than those of the previous one. For convenience of narration I shall divide them into two series: those made while the "medium" either stood upon the floor or sat upon an ordinary seat in an ordinary position; those in which she was separated from the floor, either by glass or by some object of considerable height, upon which she stood; and those in which she produced writing upon ordinary paper, said to have been dictated by the "spirits." The experiments did not always take place in the consecutive order in which I shall note them.

The report says: "The 'spirit rappings' during the evening, aside from those heard during the test with glass tumblers, were apparently confined to the floor space in the immediate vicinity of and directly beneath the table around which the company were seated."

The stenographic report of this part of the investigation proceeds as follows:

"MR. SELLERS. Is any spirit present now?

"Three raps—faint and partly distinct—are almost instantly audible. The raps apparently emanate from the floor-space directly beneath, or in the immediate vicinity of the table. This remark is applicable to all the 'rappings' during the seance at the pine table.

"The 'MEDIUM' (interpreting the sounds). That was 'yes.'

"MR. SELLERS (aside). They sounded like three.

"The raps are immediately repeated with more distinctness.

"MR. SELLERS (aside). There are three, and they are quite distinct. Is the spirit the same that was present last night?

"Three raps, apparently identical with those last heard, are again audible.

"MR. SELLERS (aside). It says it is the same spirit. I presume then, that it is Henry Seybert? (No response.) Is it Henry Seybert?

"Three raps—distinct and positive.

"MR. SELLERS. You promised last evening to

give a communication to Mr. Pepper. Are you able to communicate with him now?

"Two raps—comparitively feeble.

"The 'MEDIUM' (interpreting). One, two: that means not now.

"MR. SELLERS (repeating). Not now?

"The 'MEDIUM' (reflectively). But probably before he leaves.

"Three raps—quickly, distinctly and instantly given.

"The 'MEDIUM.' He said 'Yes, before he leaves.' (To Mr. Sellers.) You asked that question, I think?

"MR. SELLERS. Yes. Will you communicate with him before Mr. Pepper leaves to-night?

"Three raps—instantaneous, quick and vigorous."

Afterwards, the experiment of standing near a table, the "medium" not touching it, to see if sounds similar to those of the previous evening could be produced, was repeated. The "medium" insisted, however, that there should be no breaking of the circle formed about her by those who were present.

"All of the gentlemen, and the 'medium,'" says the report, "rise and remain standing. * *

"The 'MEDIUM.' This is test, something I have not gone through since I was a little child, almost.

"MR. SELLERS (after an interval of waiting). There seem to be no raps. (Another short interval.) Now Mr. Seybert, cannot you produce some raps?

"Eighty seconds here elapse with no response, when the 'medium' made an observation which was partly inaudible at the reporter's seat, the purport of which was that the 'spirit communications' are sometimes retarded or facilitated by a compliance by the listeners with certain conditions. Another interval of probably two minutes elapsed, when the 'medium' suggested to Dr. Leidy to place his hands upon the table. The suggestion was complied with.

"Mr. Sellers inquires of the 'medium' whether

a change in her position, with regard to the table, would do any good.

"'MEDIUM.' I will change positions with you.

"The change was made accordingly, but without result, and another period of waiting followed.

"The 'MEDIUM' (to Dr. Leidy). Suppose you ask some questions. You may have some friend who will respond.

"DR. LEIDY. Is any spirit present whom I know, or who knows me?

"After a pause of ten seconds, three light raps are heard.

"DR. LEIDY. Who am I?

"The 'medium' explains that the responses by rappings are mainly indicative only of affirmation or negation.

"DR. LEIDY. Will you repeat your taps to indicate that you are present yet?

"Three taps are heard.

"MR. SELLERS. Those are very clearly heard.

"The "MEDIUM' (to Dr. Leidy). Ask if that is Mr. Seybert.

"DR. LEIDY. Is Mr. Seybert present?

"Three raps—very feeble.

"DR. LEIDY (to Mr. Sellers). Was there an answer to that?

"MR. SELLERS. There was. The answer was three raps. (After an interval, in which no response is received.) There seem to be no further communications."

Later in the evening efforts to engage the defunct Mr. Seybert in conversation were again made. The company were as before gathered about the table. "Raps" were made by Mrs. Kane on the floor. The "spirit" was asked if he knew the members of the Commission present, and to state their number. When it came to the response to the latter part of the question there were "seven slow, deliberate and distinct raps."

Alas! the "spirit" had mistaken the guest of the Commission, Mr. George S. Pepper, and the stenographers for members!

The latter were seated at a separate table.

"Mr. Sellers. Are there seven members of the Committee present?

"Three raps.

"Mr. Sellers. Are they all seated around one table?

"No response. About forty seconds elapse.

"Mr. Sellers. Are they seated at two tables?

"Three raps—quite feeble.

"Mr. Sellers (to his associates). We still must go back to the one thing. The information we receive through these responses is of little importance to us compared with the information which we must obtain as to whether these sounds are produced by a disembodied Spirit or by some living person; that is, in deference to the 'Medium.' (To Mr. Furness.) Do you not think so?

"Mr. Furness is understood to assent.

"Mr. Sellers. We have tried the glass tumblers. We have the sounds here. I would ask Mrs. Kane if it is proper for us to look below the top of the table at the time the sounds are being produced, and in such a way as to see her feet.

"The 'MEDIUM.' Yes, of course, you could do that, but it is not well to break, when you are standing, suddenly. As you know, you have to conform to the rules, else you will get no rappings.

"MR. SELLERS. What are the rules?

"The 'MEDIUM' (disconnectedly.) The rules are—every test condition, that I am perfectly willing to go through, and have gone through a thousand times—at the same time, there are times when you can break the rules. So slight a thing as the disjoining of hands may break the rules. I do not think the standing on the glass has been fully tried.

"MR. SELLERS. We will try that later.

"MR. FURNESS (to the 'medium,' informally). This investigation is one of great importance to us. There is no question about it—we have heard these curious sounds. Now as to whether they come from 'spirits' or not—that would seem to be the very next logical step in our inquiry. I think you are entirely at one with us in every possible desire to have this phenomenon investigated.

"The 'MEDIUM.' Oh, certainly. But I pledge myself to conform to nothing, for—as I said in Europe—*I do not even say the sounds are from 'spirits;'* and, what is more, it is utterly beyond human power to detect them. *I do not say they are the spirits of our departed friends, but I leave others to judge for themselves.*

"MR. FURNESS. Then you have come to the conclusion that they are entirely independent of yourself.

"The 'MEDIUM.' No, *I do not know that they are entirely independent of myself.*

"MR. FURNESS. Under what conditions can you influence them?

"The response, which was partly inaudible at the reporter's seat, was understood to be: 'I cannot tell.'

"Mr. Furness. You say that in the generality of cases they are beyond your control?

"The 'Medium.' Yes.

"Mr. Furness. How in the world shall we test that?

"The 'Medium.' Well, by—

"Mr. Furness. By—what? Isolating you from the table?

"The 'Medium.' Yes.

"Mr. Furness (applying his right hand, by her permission, to the 'Medium's' head). Are you ever conscious of any vibration in your bones?

"The 'Medium.' No; but sometimes it causes an exhaustion, that is, under circumstances when the raps do not come freely.

"Mr. Furness. The freer the raps come, the better for you?

"The 'Medium.' Yes, the freer the better—the less exhaustion.

"Mr. Sellers. But do you feel now, to-night, any untoward influence operating against you?

"The 'MEDIUM.' No, not to-night, for it takes quite a little while before we feel these things.

"MR. FURNESS. Do these raps always have that vibratory sound—tr-rut—tr-rut—tr-rut?

"The 'MEDIUM.' Sometimes they vary.

"MR. FURNESS. As a general rule I have heard them sound so.

"The 'MEDIUM.' Every rap has a different sound. For instance, when the 'spirit' of Mr. Seybert rapped, if the sound was a good one, you would have noticed that his rap was different from that of another. Every one is entirely different from another.

"MR. FURNESS. Do you suppose that the present conditions are such that you can throw the raps to a part of the room other than that in which you are?

"The 'MEDIUM.' I do not pretend to do that, but I will try to do it.

" Mr. Furness and Dr. Leidy station themselves in the corner of the room, diagonally, and most remote from the pine table, at which their associates remain seated, with their hands upon the table, and 'their minds intent on having the raps produced at the corner indicated,' as requested by the 'medium,' who also remains at the table. The 'medium' asks, *'Will the " Spirit " rap at the other side of the room ?'* and, after twelve seconds, and again after forty-three seconds, repeats the inquiry. *No response is received.* The experiment is repeated with Mr. Furness and Dr. Koenig at the corner, but with a like negative result."

Let us now turn to the experiments made while the "medium" was not in a position in which her feet could touch the floor. The report says :

"Mr. Sellers made this inquiry :

"'It is proposed that the "medium" shall stand upon tumblers. Are we likely to have any demonstration ?'

"Three raps—promptly given, though feeble in delivery and but faintly audible.

"The ' MEDIUM.' There were three—a kind of tardy assent.

"Mr. Sellers (to the 'Medium'). As if the 'Spirits' might or might not communicate?

"The 'Medium.' Well, that a trial might be made.

"Three raps are here again distinctly heard—the characteristics of the sounds in this instance being rapidity and energy, or positiveness.

"The 'Medium.' That is a quick answer.

"At this point, attention is directed to the first of a series of experiments with four glass tumblers, which are placed together, with the bottoms upward, on the carpeted floor, in the center of a vacant space. The 'medium' stands directly upon these, the heels of her shoes resting upon the rear tumblers and the soles upon the front tumblers. The Committee co-operate with the 'medium,' and, in conformity with her suggestions, all the men clasp hands and form a semi-circle in front of the 'medium,' the hands of the latter being grasped by the gentlemen nearest to her on either side.

"Mr. Sellers (after a notification from the

medium to proceed). Is Mr. Seybert still present?

"No response.

"The 'MEDIUM.' It may be a few minutes before you will hear any rapping through these glasses.

"Ten seconds elapse.

"The 'MEDIUM.' This test is a very satisfactory one, if they do it. And they have done it a hundred times.

"Five seconds elapse.

"The 'MEDIUM' (to Mr. Furness). The glasses are not placed over the marble, are they?

"MR. FURNESS. No, the floor is of wood.

"MR. SELLERS (after another interval of waiting) informally remarked to Mr. Furness: 'We will wait probably for another minute to see if anything comes. As you know, the 'medium' claims that it is impossible for her to control these things—that she is merely one who is operated through.'

"Another interval expires.

"The 'MEDIUM.' That was a very faint rap. Suppose we change the position of the glasses.

"Note by the stenographer. No intimation is given that the rap here spoken of was heard by any one other than the 'medium' herself. Pursuant to the request just stated, the carpet is removed and the glass tumblers are located on the bare floor at a point about five feet distant from the place at which the test was first tried. The new location is in the center of a passage-way, about three feet in width, between a side-board on one side, and a wall projection on the other. Its selection is apparently, though not specifically, dictated by the position and movements of the 'medium.' The 'medium' and the Committee resume their positions, the former standing on the glasses and the gentlemen facing her in a group.

"The 'MEDIUM.' Now, Spirits, will you rap on the floor?

"Thirty seconds here elapsed with no response, when one glass was heard to click against the other, and the 'medium' exclaimed 'Oh!'

"The 'MEDIUM' (repeating). Will you rap on the floor?

"Thirty seconds now elapse without any demonstration.

"The 'MEDIUM' (aside). It seems to be a failure. They have done it.

"Another click of the glasses which passes without comment.

"MR. SELLERS. We will have to set down the result of the experiment on glass tumblers as negative. It may be well to try it later.

"The 'MEDIUM' (evidently reluctant to abandon the test). Suppose now, as we have gone so far, we kind of form a chain.

"The company retained their positions with hands joined, and the 'Spirits' were repeatedly requested to make their presence known. Mr. Pepper, at the suggestion of the 'medium,' asking the 'Spirit' of his friend, Henry Seybert, to manifest its presence by one rap—but all efforts to elicit such response proved ineffectual.

"When the same experiments were resumed, the lady proceeded to the space *between the sideboard and the wall*, where the last preceding test had been made, and there the tumblers were again arranged. The 'medium' resumed her position upon them, with Drs. Leidy and Koeing, and Messrs. Sellers and Furness facing her.

"The 'MEDIUM.' Will the Spirit rap here?

"Twenty-three seconds elapse.

"DR. LEIDY. Is any 'Spirit' present.

"An interval of thirty-nine seconds here followed, when the attention of the Committee was momentarily diverted by an inquiry addressed to Mr. Furness by Mr. Sellers, viz.: Whether a glass plate of sufficient strength to bear the weight of the 'medium' was procurable. At this moment the 'medium' suddenly exclaimed: 'I hear a rap. You said, "Get a glass," and there was a rap.'

"The 'MEDIUM' (repeating for the information of Mr. Furness). Somebody proposed a glass and there were three raps.

"Dr. Koenig inquires of the 'medium' whether the meaning intended to be conveyed by the sounds is that the 'spirits' desire to have the glass plate produced.

"The 'MEDIUM.' I do not know. I know there were raps. (Turning to Mr. Sellers, the 'medium' adds:) They may have been made by your heel on the floor, but certainly there were sounds.

"MR. FULLERTON. Then it was not the regular triple rap?

"The 'MEDIUM.' I could not tell.

"Just before calling attention to the alleged rap or raps, the 'medium' grasped with her right hand the wood-work of the side-board, as if for support. It was then that she stated she heard the sounds. They were apparently not heard by any one but the 'medium.'

"MR. SELLERS (addressing the 'spirit'). Will you repeat the raps we heard just now, assuming that there were some?

"Ten minutes elapse without a response.

"The 'MEDIUM.' There is no use of my standing any longer, for when they come at all, they come right away.

"MR. SELLERS (after scrutinizing the position of one of the feet of the 'medium'). The edge of the heel of the shoe rests on the back tumbler. (Assuming a stooping posture for a more prolonged scrutiny.) We will see whether the raps will be produced now.

"The 'medium' now proposes that all the members of the committee shall stand up and join hands.

"Mr. Sellers and his associates accordingly stand, facing the 'medium,' with hands joined. Changes in their positions were made by some of the gentlemen from time to time, as suggested by the 'medium,' Mr. Pepper and Dr. Koenig being the first to exchange places. This occurred after a silence of thirty seconds, without any response.

"The 'MEDIUM.' Now, Mr. Seybert, if your 'spirit' is here, will you have the kindness—I knew Mr. Seybert well in life—to rap?

"Fifteen seconds elapse.

"The 'MEDIUM.' No, he does not seem to respond.

"At the suggestion of Mr. Sellers, all of the gentlemen approach the 'medium' for the purpose of inducing some acknowledgment by the 'spirit,' and inquiries similar to those already stated are repeated without result.

"The Commission temporarily abandon the test. When the tumblers are again produced the 'medium' takes her position upon them, with Mr. Fullerton standing next to her upon the right and Mr. Furness to the left. Mr. Sellers remains for some moments kneeling on the floor to enable himself better to hear any sounds that may be but faintly audible. The 'spirits' are repeatedly importuned by the 'medium' to produce the 'rappings,' but no response is heard until the company is about to abandon the experiment. Three raps are then audible. The raps are very light, but very distinct.

"MR. FULLERTON states that he heard the raps.

"MR. SELLERS. I heard a sound then, but it

seemed as if it was around there. (Indicating the wall immediately in the rear of the 'medium.')

"The tumblers are here moved further away from the wall, and the 'medium' resumes her position upon them.

"Mr. Sellers. Will the 'Spirit' rap again? (No response.)

"The 'Medium.' Were any of you gentlemen acquainted with Mr. Seybert in his lifetime?

"Mr. Fullerton. I saw him several times before his death. If he can give an intimation now of anything he said at that time, it will indicate that he remembers it.

"A very faint rap is heard.

"The 'Medium.' There is a rap. It seems to be there again. (Indicating the spot to which attention was previously called by Mr. Sellers.)

"The 'medium' again importunes, first, 'Mr. Seybert,' and next the 'spirits,' to rap; and the importunities are repeated. Three raps are distinctly, but faintly heard.

"Mr. Sellers. I heard them. They sounded somewhat like the others, not exactly.

"The 'Medium.' I heard one rap, but it is nothing for me to hear them; I want you gentlemen to hear them.

"Mr. Sellers. Probably we will hear them again.

"While Mr. Sellers and Mr. Furness are conversing, several raps are heard, though less distinct than the preceding ones.

"The 'Medium.' There they are, as though right under the glass. (After a silence of forty seconds) Now I hear them again, very light—oh, very light.

"Mr. Furness, with the permission of the 'medium,' *places his hand upon one of her feet.*

"The 'Medium.' There are raps now, strong— yes, I hear them.

"Mr. Furness (to the 'medium'). This is the most wonderful thing of all, Mrs. Kane; *I distinctly feel them in your foot.* There is not a particle of motion in your foot, but there is an unusual pulsation.

"Mr. Sellers here made some inquiries of the 'medium,' concerning the shoes now worn by her. The replies, which were not direct, are here given.

"Mr. Sellers. Are those the shoes which you usually wear?

"The 'Medium.' I wear all kinds of shoes.

"Mr. Sellers. Are the sounds produced in your room when you have no shoes on?

"The 'Medium.' More or less. They are produced under all circumstances.

"Following the suggestion of the 'medium,' all present proceed through an intervening apartment to the library, where the 'medium' selects various positions—standing upon a lounge, then upon a cushioned chair, next upon a stepladder, and finally upon the side of a book-case—but all with a like unsuccessful result, no response by 'rappings' being heard.

"In the midst of the experiments at the table Mrs. Kane exclaimed to Mr. Sellers: Well, my hand does feel like writing. Will you give me a piece of paper? and, maybe they will give me some directions.

"Mr. Fullerton (to the 'medium'). How does your hand feel when affected in that way?

"The 'Medium.' It is a peculiar feeling, like that from taking hold of electrical instruments. I do not know but that you might possibly feel it in my hand.

"The lady here extended her right hand upon the table toward Mr. Fullerton. The latter placed his left hand upon the extended hand of the 'medium,' and subsequently remarked that the pulsation of her wrist was a little above the ordinary rate.

"The 'medium,' ostensibly under 'spirit' influence, with lead-pencil in hand, proceeded to write two communications from the 'spirit' of the late Henry Seybert. The first of these covered two pages of paper of the size of ordinary foolscap. The 'medium' wrote in large characters, with remarkable rapidity, and in a direction from the right to the left, or the reverse of ordinary handwriting. The writing, consequently, could be read only from the reverse side of the paper, and by being held up so as to permit the gaslight to shine through it.

"The communications, as deciphered by Mr. Sellers, with the aid of Mr. Fullerton and the 'medium,' were as follows :

"You must not expect that I can satisfy you beyond all doubt in so short a time as you have yet had. I want to give you all in my power, and will do so if you will give me a chance. You must commence right in the first place or you shall all be disappointed for a much longer time. *Princiipis Obsta Sereo Medicina Paratum.*
"HENRY SEYBERT.
"Mend the fault in time or we will all be puzzled.
"HENRY SEYBERT."

The fault in the Latin of the above quotation attracted the attention of the Commission.

Mr. George S. Pepper, who had been well acquainted with Mr. Seybert in his lifetime, declared that he had never known any Latin at all!

The investigations of the "Seybert Commission" in other directions than that of the "rappings," were far more fascinating and productive of results. It would be impossible to give an adequate idea of them here. The Commission employed the most celebrated "mediums" within their reach, and paid them liberally to place them in communication with the "Spirit world." They saw (and they show in their report that they did see) the secret of every "wonderful" thing done by the "mediums," and found it in most instances exceedingly simple, and generally rather clumsily performed. Professional jugglers constantly outdo professional "mediums." This, the latter cannot deny, and they seek—oh, monumental impudence!—to make people believe that jugglers are nothing more nor less than "mediums," and that "mediums" are never in any sense jugglers!

Thus the notorious Slade:

"MR. SELLERS. Do you know a man named Kellar, who is exhibiting in this city?

"DR. SLADE. I do not. I never knew him.

"MR. SELLERS. You may, however, be able to explain to me a very remarkable slate writing experiment which Kellar has performed. (Mr. Sellers here describes at length Mr. Kellar's trick with the fastened slates.) How did Mr. Kellar do that?

"DR. SLADE. He is a 'medium.' *He does that work precisely as I do it.*

"MR. SELLERS. But can he not do it by trickery?

"DR. SLADE. No, it is impossible. He is a 'medium' and a powerful 'medium.'"

This is from a memorandum of Mr. Sellers. He says further:

"The inquiry was then addressed to Mr. Slade: Do you know a man named Guernilla, who, with his wife, gave séances?

"MR. SLADE. Yes, I know him very well.

"MR. SELLERS. Well, how does he perform his wonderful exploits in 'rappings,' etc.?

"MR. SLADE. He is a 'medium,' a powerful 'medium.' I know him very well indeed. I can assure you that all he does is done solely by means of his mediumistic powers.

"I now state to the Committee that the Guernillas exhibited in Philadelphia some years ago as exposers of Spiritualism. They did not expose it, but they performed experiments which, prior to that time, were said to have been accomplished by the aid of 'spirits.' Guernilla himself, at my house, in my presence, in broad daylight, performed all the feats and exhibited the phenomena that were produced at the dark and other séances, and he repeated them until I myself became as expert as he in performing them; for which I paid him a consideration. So much for the mediumistic power."

Mr. Sellers explained with reference to Mr. Kellar:

"I pause here for the express purpose of having the fact noted that, being thoroughly familiar with the details of the methods of those experiments, I can positively assure the Committee that there is no mediumistic power in Mr. Kellar, so far as his methods are concerned, that those methods are as easy of solution as are any other physical problems."

CHAPTER XIII.

THE UNALTERABLE VERDICT.

The "Seybert Commission"* examined every known form of spiritualistic manifestation to which they had access, and implicitly under conditions imposed by the "mediums" themselves. These conditions are everything that could be devised and plausibly used to prevent the hoped-for dupe from detecting the fraud that is practised upon him.

The Commission put the indelible stamp of fraud upon all so-called spiritualistic manifestations. Of the "spiritual rappings" they say:

"To the subject of 'spirit-rappings' we have devoted some time and attention, but our investi-

---

* "The Seybert Commission on Spiritualism," J. B. Lippincott Company, Philadelphia, 1887. The author is under obligations to the publishers of this volume, for material which he has taken from it.

gations have not been sufficiently extensive to warrant us at present in offering any positive conclusions. The difficulty attending the investigation of this mode of spiritualistic manifestation is increased by the fact, familiar to physiologists, that sounds of varying intensity may be produced in almost any portion of the human body by voluntary muscular action. To determine the exact location of this muscular activity is at times a matter of delicacy.

"What we can say thus far, with assurance, is that, in the cases which have come under our observation, the theory of the purely physiological origin of the sounds has been sustained by the fact that the 'mediums' were invariably, and confessedly, cognizant of the 'rappings' whenever they occurred, and could at once detect any spurious 'rappings,' however exact and indistinguishable to all other ears might be the imitation."

Mrs. Kane has expressed amusement over the manner in which she eluded the inquisitions of the grave and conscientious Commission and left them puzzled over the "rappings."

Even then, however, she cared so little for the preservation of the secret, that when she declined to be further examined by the Commission, she admitted to Mr. Furness that the gentlemen had ample ground for looking upon the manifestations which she had given as unsatisfactory. Mr. Furness says:

"I told her that the Commission had now had two séances with her, and that *the conclusion to which they had come is that the so-called raps are confined wholly to her person*, whether produced by her voluntarily or involuntarily they had not attempted to decide; furthermore, that although thus satisfied in their own minds they were anxious to treat her with all possible deference and consideration, and accordingly had desired me to say to her that if she thought another séance with her would or might modify or reverse their conclusion, they held themselves ready to meet her again this evening and renew the investigation of the manifestations; at the same time I felt it my duty to add that in that case the examination would necessarily be of the most searching description.

"Mrs. Kane replied that the manifestations at both séances had been of an unsatisfactory nature, so unsatisfactory that *she could not really blame the Commission for arriving at their conclusion.* In her present state of health she *really* doubted whether a third meeting would prove any better than the two already held. It might even be more unsatisfactory, and instead of removing the present belief of the Commission it might add confirmation of it. In view of these considerations, she decided not to hold another séance."

Mrs. Kane declares that with her muscles and the joints of her toes so educated by long practice, and her ability to produce the noise of "raps" with no perceptible movement, she could have gone on deceiving the world indefinitely without being detected. She explains that the making of the "raps," when she is stationed on glass tumblers, requires a far greater effort than when her feet are in contact with the carpet or floor. The shock must in that case be conveyed through a comparatively non-conducting substance. For this reason, when the floor was especially hard or thick and lacking in sonorousness, she sometimes failed in the expected effect. In every instance, it was most difficult to produce the "raps" under those circumstances.

The verdict, however, is now complete. Spiritualism is guilty.

The court of mankind so declares it.

IV.
REPENTANCE.

CHAPTER XIV.

THE HEART PLEADS FOR THE SOUL.

The most interesting feature, after all, of Margaret Fox's career, was perhaps that sad and abortive romance of which Dr. Elisha Kent Kane, the gallant Arctic explorer, was the hero. This history should be known to the reader in order that the exact aspect of Spiritualism to her developed conscience in after years may be understood.

Dr. Kane first saw Maggie Fox in the autumn of 1852, when she was staying with her mother at a hotel in Philadelphia, being then engaged in "spiritualistic manifestations." Dr. Kane, whose heart had never before been touched, at once succumbed to the sweet charm of this erratic child, and conceived the romantic idea of removing her from the life she then was leading, educating her and marrying her. The project, when it became known, awakened the bitter hostility of his friends, and from this hostility, the unfortunate separation between them which it caused, and Dr. Kane's untimely death, all of the sorrow that afterwards engulfed her life and deprived her of the ambition for a nobler career, directly sprang.

Margaret was but thirteen years old when Dr. Kane first saw her. A friendly hand[*] has thus traced her portrait :

" Her beauty was of that delicate kind which grows on the heart, rather than captivates the sense at a glance ; she possessed in a high degree that retiring modesty which shuns rather than seeks admiration. The position in which she was placed imposed on her unusual reserve and self-control, and an ordinary observer might not have seen in her aught to make a sudden impression. But there was more than beauty in the charm

[*] The author of " The Love-Life of Dr. Kane ;" published by Carleton, 1865, New York.

about her discerned by the penetrating eyes of her new acquaintance. The winning grace of her modest demeanor, and the native refinement apparent in every look and movement, word and tone, were evidences of a nature enriched with all the qualities that dignify and adorn womanhood; of a soul far above her present calling, and those who surrounded her. To appreciate her real superiority, her age and the circumstances must be considered. She was yet a little child—untutored, except in the elements of instruction to be gained in country district schools, when it was discovered that she possessed a mysterious power,* for which no science or theory could account. This brought her at once into notoriety and gathered around her those who had a fancy for the supernatural, and who loved to excite the wonder of strangers. Most little girls would

---

* This form of expression was here used because the author of "The Love-Life," while not a believer in Spiritualism, did not wish to imply in a work that had Mrs. Kane's personal sanction, the slightest doubt of the sincerity of her professions or of her claims as a "medium."

have been spoiled by that kind of attention. The endurance of it without having her head turned, argued rare delicacy, simplicity and firmness of character. After exhibitions given in different cities, to find herself an object of public attention, and of flattering notice from persons of distinction, would naturally please the vanity of a beautiful young girl; and it would not be surprising if a degree of self-conceit were engendered. But Margaret was not vain, and could not be made self-conceited. If she had any consciousness of her exquisite loveliness,—if it pleased her to possess pretty dresses and ornaments—her delight was that of a happy child taking pleasure in beautiful things, without reference to any effect they might enable her to produce. Perhaps no young girl ever lived more free from the least idea of coquetry or conquest. She heeded not the expressions of admiration that reached her ear so frequently. She had seen enough of the world at this time to be aware of the advantages of a superior education, and it was the most ardent wish of her heart to make herself a well-educated woman."

Margaret showed a disposition to devote herself with great industry to the acquirement of knowledge. In fact, at her first meeting with Dr. Kane, he found her conning over a French exercise in an interval of the public receptions which were given by herself and her mother. Dr. Kane easily enlisted her thoughts in a better and higher career. The deception which was required of her already appeared in something of its true light to her young mind, and she was restless under its abhorrent shackles. Dr. Kane's interest in her was certainly pure and elevated, and it led him to gloomy apprehensions of the fate of so fair, yet so misguided, a creature. He wrote in verse a prophecy that she would "live and die forlorn." There have been many times when the latter part of this warning seemed most likely to come true; and that, doubtless, would have been her fate had she not found in a final renunciation of her past, a solace to her heart for the lack of that falsely won prosperity which had been hers during but brief intervals.

Dr. Kane was but an indifferent versifier; but some of the trifles in rhyme which he addressed to Margaret may well illustrate certain facts that I shall state at length hereafter. One day, he sent her "Thoughts that Ought to Be Those of Maggie Fox," the first refrain of which is as follows:

> "Dreary, dreary, dreary,
> Passes life away,
> Dreary, dreary, dreary,
> The day
> Glides on, and *weary*
> *Is my hypocrisy.*"

At the close of the second stanza were these lines:

> "Happy as the hopes
> Which filled my trusting heart,
> Before I knew a sinful wish
> Or learned *a sinful art.*"

Again :

> "So long this secret have I kept
> I can't forswear it now.
> It festers in my bosom,
> It cankers in my heart,
> *Thrice cursed is the slave fast chained
> To a deceitful art !*"

And last :

> "Then the maiden knelt and prayed:
> 'Father, my anguish see ;
> Oh, give me but one trusting hope
> Whose heart will shelter me ;
> One trusting love to share my griefs,
> To snatch me from a life forlorn ;
> That I may never, never, never,
> Thus endlessly from night to morn,
> Say that *my life is dreary
> With its hypocrisy !*"

Among the first words that Dr. Kane spoke to Margaret were these : "This is no life for you, my child." As their reciprocal attraction grew stronger, he bent all of his deep influence over her in one direction, to effect once and for all her release from the fatal snare of deceit that fate had cast about her. Only a few weeks later we find him writing her a note from New York, in which he says:

"Look at the *Herald* of this morning. There is an account of a suicide which causes some excitement. Your sister's* name is mentioned in the inquest of the coroner. Oh, how much I wish that you would quit *this life of dreary sameness and unsuspected deceit.* We live in this world only for the good and noble. How crushing it must be to occupy with them a position of ambiguous respect!"

Dr. Kane, a short time afterwards, described Maggie as follows:

"But it is that strange mixture of child and woman, of simplicity and cunning, of passionate impulse and extreme self-control, that has made you a curious study. Maggie, you are very pretty, very childlike, very deceitful, but to me as readable as my grandmother's Bible."

* Leah.

"And again he said : "When I think of you, dear darling, *wasting your time and youth and conscience for a few paltry dollars*, and think of the crowds who come nightly to hear of the wild stories of the frigid North, I sometimes feel that we are not so far removed after all. My brain and your body are each the sources of attraction, and I confess that there is not so much difference."

Never for an instant did the manly and robust intellect of Dr. Kane stoop to the level of even a partial belief in the pretended wonders of "Spiritualism." The allusions made to it in his letters, when not grave or indignant, are full of a certain contemptuous playfulness, well calculated to reprove the conscious deceitfulness practised by the childish Maggie, while not offending the natural pride which was yet a part of her imperfectly formed character. When the doctor was in Boston, he wrote to her sister Katie :

"Well, now for talk. Boston is a funny place, and 'the spirits' have friends here. You would be surprised if I told you what I have heard. * * * There are some things that I have seen which I think would pain you. Maggie would only laugh at them; but with me it gave cause for sadness. I saw a young man with a fine forehead and expressive face, but a countenance deeply tinged with melancholy, seize the hand of this 'medium,' whose name—as I never tell other's secrets—I cannot tell you. He begged her to answer a question which I could not hear. Instantly she rapped, and his face assumed a positive agony; the rapping continued; his pain increased; I leaned forward, feeling an utter detestation for the woman who could inflict such torment; but it was too late. A single rap came and he fell senseless in a fit. This I saw with my own eyes.

"Now, Katie, although you and Maggie have never gone so far as this, yet circumstances must occur where you have to lacerate the feelings of other people. I know that you have a tender heart; but practice in anything hardens us. You do things now which you would never have dreamed of doing years ago ; and there will come a time when you will be worse than Leah ; a hardened woman, gathering around you *the victims of a delusion.* * * * The older you grow the more difficult it will be to liberate yourself from this thing. And can you look forward to a life unblessed by the affections, unsoothed by the consciousness of doing right ! * * * *When your mother leaves this scene, can you and * * Maggie be content to live that life of constant deceit ?*"

To Maggie, Dr. Kane wrote from the sincerest depths of his heart, recalling the first moment when he saw her, "a little Priestess, cunning in the mysteries of her temple, and weak in everything but the power with which she played her part. A sentiment almost of pity stole over his wordly heart as he saw through the disguise."

And again : "Waddy * called on me to-day, as did Tallmadge ;† I was kind to both for your

---

* General Waddy Thompson.   † Ex-Governor Tallmadge.

sake. Waddy talked much about you. He said that he feared for you, and spoke long and well upon the dangers and temptations of your present life. I said little to him other than my convictions of your own and your sister's excellent character and '*pure simplicity;*' for thus, Mag, I always talk of you. And it pained me to find that others viewed your life as I did, and regarded you as occupying an ambiguous position. Depend upon it, Maggie, no right-minded gentleman—whether he be believer or sceptic—can regard your present life with approval. Let this, dear sweet, make you think over the offer of the one friend who would stretch out an arm to save you. Think wisely, dear darling, ere it be too late.
* * *

"Maggie, you cannot tell the sadness that comes over me when I think of you. What will become of you? you, the one being that I regard even before myself! * * *

"If you really can make up your mind to

abjure the spirits, to study and improve your mental and moral nature, it may be that a career of brightness will be open to you ; and upon this chance, slender as it is, I offer, like a true friend, to guard and educate you. But, Mag, clouds, and darkness rest upon the execution of your good resolves ; and I sometimes doubt whether you have the firmness of mind to carry them through."

The author of "The Love-Life of Dr. Kane," says of this period :

"Dr. Kane was very often in the habit of saying—as if with melancholy presentiment—'What would become of you if I should die? What would you do? I shudder at the thought of my death, on your account.'

"In the buoyant confidence of youth, the poor girl could not then understand his fears. But *he* knew that in separating her from Spiritualism he was isolating her from all her friends and associates, and depriving her of the only means she possessed of earning a livelihood. In compensation for the sacrifices required of her, he was giving her a hope only ; a hope that might be blissfully realized, but might be sadly disappointed ; and in the event of losing him, what must be her destiny !"

Dr. Kane met with malignant opposition from Leah, Maggie's elder sister, in his efforts to detach her from the damning career into which she had been thrown. The "shekels" were then pouring in in great abundance at the séances, and this explains sufficiently the hostile attitude of the one person who was chiefly responsible for the ruin of her young life. Thus the doctor wrote to Maggie in New York :

"Is the old house dreary to you? * * * Oh, Maggie, are you never tired of *this weary, weary sameness of continual deceit?* Are you thus to spend your days, doomed never to rise to better things ?—you and that dear little open-minded sister Kate (for she, too, is still unversed in deception)—are you both to live on thus forever? You will never be happy if you do; for you are not, like Leah, able to exult and take pleasure in the simplicity of the poor, simple-hearted fools around you.

"Do, then, Maggie, keep to your last promise. Show this to Katie, and urge her to keep to her resolution."*

By this time, Maggie had pledged herself to her lover to abandon the "rappings" altogether; but they were both very cautious lest this resolution should be known to her elder sister. Maggie appears to have yielded to the influences around her, in spite of her respect and regard for the doctor, and once or twice to have lapsed back into the ways that he dreaded and abhorred. We find him then, writing from New York to Washington:

"Don't rap for Mrs. Pierce.† Remember your promise to me. * * *

---

*Katie, as well as her sister, had promised to abjure the "spirits," and she had also said that she would go to live with Maggie on the latter's marriage with Dr. Kane.
† The wife of the President of the United States.

"Begin again, dearest Maggie, and keep your word. No 'rapping' for Mrs. Pierce or ever more for any one. I, dear Mag, am your best, your truest, your only friend. What are they to my wishes? Oh, regard and love me, and listen to my words; and be very careful lest in an idle hour you lose my regard and your own respect."

And later:

"All last night did this good friend of yours think about you and your probable future.

"I can see that this is one of the turning points of your life, and upon your own energy and decision now depend the success and happiness of your future career. Dear Maggie, think it over well and *do not be turned aside from what is right* by the sincere but still misguided advice of others. * * * But remember, Maggie, that all this will not last. * * * What will it be when, looking back upon * * * misspent and dreary years, you feel that there have been no acts really acceptable to your Maker, and that for the years ahead, all will be sorrow, sameness and disgust! * * *

"Why, you know that sometimes, even now, when Leah is cross, or the company coarse and vulgar, or the day tiresome, or yourself out of sorts, that low spirits and disgust come over you and you long like a bird to spread your wings and fly away from it all."

Very soon afterwards, Dr. Kane wrote:

"At present, you have nothing to look forward to, nothing to hope for. Your life is one constant round of idle excitement. Can your mother, who is an excellent woman, look upon you, a girl of thirteen, as doomed all your life to live surrounded by such as now surround you, *deprived of all the blessings of home and love and even self-respect?*"

Dr. Kane, looking upon Margaret as his future wife, was exceedingly anxious that the true explanation of the "rappings," the fact that they were entirely fraudulent, should never be discovered. He hoped that Spiritualism would have but an ephemeral existence, and that when once it had died out, the public would so far forget the persons who originated it, that it would cease to associate with them the woman who would then bear his name. So he wrote in this vein to Maggie:

"You know I am nervous about the 'rappings.' I believe the only thing I ever was afraid of was this confounded thing being found out. I would not know it myself for ten thousand dollars."

How both Margaret and Dr. Kane regarded the elder sister may be judged from this sentence, written by the latter at this time: "Be careful not to mention me before the Tigress."

At last the object dearest to Dr. Kane's heart seemed to be drawing near to its accomplishment. He says: "Your kind promise 'solemnly never to rap again' so pleases me, that I cannot help thanking you. Adhere to that, and you will be a dear, good, happy girl." * * *

Maggie went to school at Crookville, near

Chester, Pennsylvania, and was in charge of Dr. Kane's aunt, Mrs. Leiper, who resided near the house where Maggie lodged. Just prior to this, Dr. Kane wrote as follows:

"*Never do wrong any more; for if now 'the spirits move' it will be a breach of faith. From this moment, our compact begins.*"

After Dr. Kane had reached the Arctic seas, I find this passage at the end of a long letter, full of solicitude and noble counsel about the education of his future wife: "One final wish—the only thing like restraint that your true friend can find it in his heart to utter: See little of Leah, and never sleep within her house."

For a short time, on his return from his second Arctic voyage, Dr. Kane allowed himself to be swayed by interest and the vehement efforts of his relatives, so far as to require from Margaret a written declaration that they had never been engaged, and that she had no claim whatever upon his hand in matrimony. There was a quick reaction, however, and the old relations were renewed. One who wrote of these facts said: Amid all his sorrow, one fear seemed to harass him perpetually—that Miss Fox might be induced to return to the professional life she had abandoned years ago for his sake. She was surrounded by spiritualists." * * *

In his letters to her, Dr. Kane still harped upon the one anxiety that continually possessed him. He says: "*Do avoid 'spirits.' I cannot bear to think of you as engaged in a course of wickedness and deception.* * * * Pardon my saying so; but is it not deceit even to listen when others are deceived? * * * In childhood it was a mere indiscretion; but what will it be when hard age wears its wrinkles into you, and like Leah you grow old! Dear Maggie, I could cry to think of it. * * * A time will come when you will see the real ghost of memory—an awful specter!"

And again he wrote: "*Maggie, I have but one thought,* how to make you happier; *how to with-*

draw you from deception; from a course of sin and future punishment, the dark shadow of which hung over you like the wing of a vampire."

Then, as he claimed her more and more openly as his own, "he would not permit her," says the writer already quoted, "even to witness any spiritual manifestations, nor to remain in the room when the subject was discussed. * * * 'You never shall be brought in contact with such things again,' he would say."

The ending of this very sad tale of love, which throws a peculiar light athwart the colder theme of this volume, was bitterly tragic. A secret marriage under the common law was entered into, and Dr. Kane, whose health was shattered never to be mended, went first to Europe and then to Cuba to die. Margaret and her mother were to join him at Havana, but ere their departure from New York he was already a corpse.

And so, a noble and generous, if sometimes faltering heart, ceased to beat, and a gentle creature, who at last had learned to love as much as she had honored him, was on the shores of that deep sea of infamy against which, had he only lived, he would surely have shielded her.

CHAPTER XV.

FROM SHADOW TO LIGHT.

More than thirty years after this sorrowful event, Margaret Fox Kane, in reviewing the past, attributes to the evil of Spiritualism all the ill-fortune which afterwards befell her.

For fourteen years she wore the weeds of mourning for his sake; but when at last they were torn from her by a friendly, though unwise hand, she drifted again, through the various phases of a worldly and dissipated life, to that very vocation of dreary mercenary deceit which he had predicted would be her lot. She was never happy afterwards, however, and he who possesses any true sensibility must at least pity, quite as much as he may condemn her unfortunate destiny, when he reads the sad avowals which are made in this volume.

Mrs. Kane says at the present day:

"From the very first of our intimate acquaintance, Dr. Kane knew that the 'rappings' which I practiced were fraudulent. Of course, he was too keen-sighted intellectually, too sensible, ever to have believed them genuine for a single instant; and I simply obeyed the impulse of my candid regard for him, when the knowledge of his devotion grew upon me, and confided to him the whole secret of the fraud, together with my increasing repugnance to the life I was leading. He hated it, he despised it, he abhorred it, and he taught me from the beginning the same sentiment. We had to combat with the sordid interest of others. Whatever good he accomplished for me, was done against the set purpose of Leah.

"I do not exaggerate in any way when I say that I have feared that woman all my life. Remember, she is twenty-three years older than I am. Her influence over both myself and my sister Kate began when we were infants. Katie, even to this day, acknowledges some sinister influence about her sister Leah, even if she but chance to meet her in the street. It is a mixture of terrorism and cajolery.

"For years I have had the shame of this vile thing before me. All my life, it has made me miserable. It is a load which I now throw off with a free heart and a great and thrilling sense of relief

"You must know that it was a dark and hateful influence that kept me aloof from Dr. Kane so long, when he declared his true love for me, over and over again, and desired to rescue me from the evil by which I was surrounded. I gave him my whole heart in return, though at that time I did not know how deep and how tender was my love for him.

"It is this same baleful influence which has been the nightmare of my existence. Every morning of my life on awaking, I have had this horrid thought before me And even in those younger days I would brood and brood over it, and Dr. Kane would often say to me:

"'Maggie, I see the vampire is hovering over you still.'

"Our whole family was at that time under bondage, as it were, to Ann Leah Brown. She ruled over us as with a rod of iron.

"All through this dreadful life—from the time when I first realized its enormity—I protested against it. Dr. Kane, after our marriage, would never permit me to allude to my old career—he wanted me to forget it. He hated its publicity.

"But when I was poor after his death, I was driven back to it. I have told my sister Leah over and again: 'Now that you are rich, why don't you save your soul? But she would only fly into a passion. The truth is that nothing can excuse the work she has done. She entered upon it at the age of judgment and experience, fully aware of its falsity and evil effect. She knows that the world cannot forgive her, and I have no hope that she will ever confess her sin, or offer an atonement for it.

"What can I add to the revelations of those

letters? They are proofs of the mutual knowledge of Dr. Kane and myself that the 'spiritual' rappings' were fraud, and nothing but fraud. And even if he had not been told of the fact by myself, his opportunities of observation in our household were unequaled by any granted to others, and his verdict would have been in any case, therefore, almost as authoritative.

"What fools are they who still pretend to believe against all this evidence!

"It would hardly seem necessary that I should denounce Spiritualism after all that others have said against it.

"I have never in my life professed to be a spiritualist, and I have never believed in Spiritualism, although I have seen it in all its phases, some of which I am unable to produce myself.

"Even when I was compelled to go back to the 'rappings' for a livelihood, and when I charged the most exorbitant fees, so that as few people as possible might be deceived, I had on my cards an emphatic disclaimer of any occult inspiration.

Mrs. Kane at this point showed the following on the back of one of her cards :

> Mrs. Kane does not claim any Spirit power; but people must judge for themselves.

"My poor father and mother," she continued, "both knew before their death that all that we had practised for so many years was a fraud and a deception. Mother was greatly troubled about it, and she turned to the church for comfort. She used to say to us:

"'Oh, my dear children, I do hope that you will get out of this sort of life soon.'

"Peace be unto her!"

―――

The evil effects of Spiritualism upon the moral and mental condition of its followers is the deepest stain upon its history. The wrecks of thousands of intellects are monuments to its heartless fraud and malign influence.

Mrs. Kane has often said that if in her late years she had wholly submitted herself to its foolish vagaries and its base temptations, she would undoubtedly be now a raving maniac.

There are many who, if they would but speak truly, could declare that ruin of conscience, brain and health, has resulted either from their willing faith in flimsy illusions or their weak connivance in puerile deception.

I have touched but little upon the unclean side of Spiritualism. Thousands upon thousands of virtuous men and women entertain its theory or hold to its faith. But the manipulators of the supernatural machinery, the members of the inner circle, the prestidigitateurs and clumsy magicians, who seek to make simpletons of mankind, I now accuse of the grossest practices and abominations, the loosest social ideas, the most utter absence of principle that has been exhibited by any one set of people in the nineteenth century.

They are wholly corrupt, and there is no good in them.

If Spiritualism in any form survives the blow now given it by Margaret and Catherine Fox, who were its creators, it will only be because of the veiled licentiousness introduced into it by those who have enlarged upon its original plan.

This licentiousness, like the bruised serpent, will not down, but still will lift its head, and lurk amid deepest shadows.

Spiritualism, however, cannot again deceive the world.

And it is written :

"The dead shall not return ; nor any that go down into Hell !"

INDEX.

INDEX

INDEX.

ABJURATION by Margaret Fox Kane of Spiritualism at the Academy of Music, New York, 65, 74.
ADMISSIONS of Mrs. Leah Fox Fish regarding the results of the Buffalo medical investigation, 140, 144.
AGASSIZ (Professor) investigates Spiritualism, 147.
ANTICS of the Fox Children at Hydesville near Rochester, 83, 87, 89, 96.
ATTRACTIONS of the younger Fox Sisters, 129.
AUDACITY (Imbecile) of spiritualistic imposters, 146.—(Supreme) of fraud, 150.
AUTHORIZATION of the publication of this work by Margaret Fox Kane and Catherine Fox Jencken, 7.
"BABY mediumship"—How the trick was done with the child of Mrs. Catherine Fox Jencken, 160.
BELIEF in Spiritualism,—Mrs. Kane never pretended to any, 167, 181, 236.—John D. Fox never had any, 99.
"BOBBING" of apples on the floor in the Hydesville house, 84, 90, 95.
BOOMERANGS (Spiritualistic), 131.
BROWN (Mrs. Ann Leah Fox),—Malignant opposition to Dr. Kane's efforts to detach her sister Maggie from Spiritualism, 222, 232.—Exulting in deception, 223.—Maggie warned against her by Dr. Kane, 227.—Sinister influence over her sisters, 232.
'BUFFALO Doctors"—Their investigation of the "rappings," 131.—Their correct theory, but wrong hypothesis, 131.—

How their investigation if further pursued, would have led to the truth 133.
"CHARLES Ceri"—The "spirit of Mr. Seybert" mistakes the name of Mr. Sellers, of the "Seybert Commission," 171.
CLAIMS of Spiritualism as set forth in petition to Congress, 1854, 151, 152.
COMMITTEES of tools and accomplices, 121.
CONDEMNATION of Spiritualism—The substantial effect of the report of Harvard professors on the tests in Boston, 1857, 149.
CONCERTED signals used in the early séances, 127.
CONSPICUOUS persons interested in the "Fox Sisters," 129.
CONTACT of person while producing the "raps," 90, 138.
CORRUPT practices in secret spiritualistic circles, 50, 64, 237.
COVENTRY (Dr. C. B.), one of the Buffalo investigators, 132.
CROOKVILLE, near Philadelphia—Maggie Fox goes to school there, 226.
DEAD (The) do not return, 37, 238.
DEATH of Dr. Kane, 37.
DERANGEMENT of mental faculties the cause of the prevalence of the spiritualistic delusion, 154.—Resulting from Spiritualism, 166.
DISGUST (Dr. Kane's) at spiritualistic circles, 225, 229.—(Mrs. Kane's) at the baser spiritualistic practices, 29, 30.
DISS De Bar (Madam)—Mrs. Kane's abhorrence of her, 29.—Daniel Underhill pronounces her a fraud, 43.
EARLY sorcery the prototype of modern Spiritualism, 150.
EDUCATION (Defective) the cause of the prevalence of the spiritualistic delusion, 154.
ELEVATION—Failure of Mrs. Kane to produce "rappings" when standing upon a lounge, a cushioned chair or a step-ladder, 195.
EXPOSURE, Poetic justice of the, 13.—Mrs. Kane's first public intimation of intended, 29, 30.—Details of Mrs. Kane's, 32, 35, 37, 65, 77.—Of Spiritualism by the Guernillas, 199.

FEAR of the Fox Sisters of their sister, Leah, 232.
FISH (Ann Leah Fox) First to conceive the idea of profiting by the "rappings," 102.—Learns to "rap" from the little children, 103.—Using the little girls, Maggie and Katie, for her purposes, 123.—Challenges to the "Buffalo doctors," 139.
FISH (Lizzie)—Protesting against her mother's hypocrisy and deception, 96, 128.
FLINT (Dr. Austin), one of the Buffalo investigators, 132.
FOOT (Movement of the) in producing "rappings," 38, 103, 143. —Detected by a member of the "Seybert Commission," 194.—"Rappings" not heard when held, but heard again when released, 143.
FORGED testimony, 91.
FOX (Catherine)—First to discover that "raps" could be produced with the joints, 90.
FOX (David S.)—First to suggest use of the alphabet in the so-called "spirit messages," 115.—Dupe or accomplice of Leah, 115.
FOX (John D.)—Never a believer in Spiritualism, 99.
FOX (Mrs. Margaret)—An honest fanatic, deceived by her children, 36, 93.—Disabused at the last, 236.
FOX (Maggie)—Her beauty at thirteen years, 210.—Petty devilment in childhood, 83.—Sent to school at Crookville, Pa., by Dr. Kane, 226.—Protests all through her earlier life against "spiritualistic" deception, 234.
FOX (Maria), 82.
FULCRUM, necessary for the limb in order to produce sound by the action of the joints, 142.
FURNESS (Horace Howard), acting chairman of the "Seybert Commission"—Letter to Mrs. Kane, 169.—Explanation of her refusal to continue the séances with the Commission, 204.
FRAUD—Dante's image of, 17.—Origin of the, 81.—Development of the, 105.—Various forms of the, 201.

FRAUDULENT—The "mediumship" of Mrs. Jencken's baby, "Ferdie," 160.
GARBLED testimony, 90, 94.
"GOD has not ordered it," 25, 37.
GOWNS (Long) put on the younger Fox girls on their first public appearance, to conceal manner of producing "raps," 123.
GREELEY (Horace)—Aids Katie, 19, 58, 129.—Influence upon her life, 129.
GUERNILLAS (The)—Exposure of Spiritualism, 199.
"HERALD" (The N. Y.), 25, 28, 29, 32, 39, 42, 46, 62.
HISTORY of the "rappings," 79.
HARVARD professors investigate Spiritualism, 147.
HUMBUG (Spiritualism a,) according to Mrs. Kate Fox Jencken, 57.
HYDESVILLE, N. Y.—When mysterious sounds were first heard in John D. Fox's house, 81.—Digging in the creek, 95.—Bones of a horse found, 118.—Digging in the cellar, 117.—Alleged finding of human bones, unconfirmed by any evidence, 117.—House said to be haunted—an afterthought, 101.—The "spirits" when asked tentatively say a murder was committed in the house and mention the name of the murderer, 119.
HYPOCRISY of professional spiritualists, 165.—Dr. Kane characterizes, 214, 215.
INQUISITIVENESS as to spiritualistic methods prevents the "spirits" from acting, 146.
INSULATION—Experiments with Mrs. Kane while standing on glass tumblers, 185.—The results negative, 188.—Partial success when placed near a sideboard and wall, 189, 192.
INVESTIGATION—First farcical, 122, 124.—By the "Buffalo doctors," 131, 134.—By "Buffalo doctors" again, 131.—By "Seybert Commission," 170.—By Harvard professors and others, 147.
JENCKEN (Mrs. Catherine Fox) denounces Spiritualism, 62, 64.

JOINTS of the fingers.—Children try to imitate sounds with them, 87.
JOINT of the knee used in the production of "raps," 133.
JOINTS of the toes used in producing the famous "rappings" of the Fox sisters, 139, 145.
JUGGLERY—Spiritualists attribute it to "mediumship," 198.— Confess that "spiritualistic" effects are produced in the same way, 199.—Older and more skillful than Spiritualism so-called, 150, 154.
KANE (Dr. Elisha Kent)—First meeting with Maggie Fox, 209.— Influence upon her life, 129.—Effect of his death on her career, 230, 231.—Character of his interest in her, 213.— Gloomy foresight, 213.—Efforts to save her from a life of fraud, &c., 129, 228.—Characterizes the deceit and hypocrisy of "mediumship," 214, 215, 216, 228.—Never believed in a single pretense of Spiritualism, 217, 232.— Knew from their first acquaintance that the "rappings" were fraudulent, 232.—Repeatedly exacts her promise not to have anything more to do with Spiritualism, 223, 226.—Solicitude lest she return to the practice of Spiritualism, 228.—Fear lest the source of the "rappings" be discovered, 226.—Places her at school, 226.—Engagement broken off and renewed, 227.—Secret marriage with her, 229.—Death at Havana, 229.
KNEES—Seized by investigators to detect movement while "rappings" being produced, 143.—When so seized, sounds arrested, and when released, renewed, 143.
LEE (Dr. Charles A.), one of the Buffalo investigators, 132.
LETTER of Mrs. Kane first publicly denouncing Spiritualism, 30.
LICENTIOUSNESS under the cloak of Spiritualism, 237, 238.
"MEDIUMS" (Well-known)—How they received the exposé, 45, 46.
"MEDIUMSHIP"—Mrs. Kane driven back to it, 37.
MESSAGES (Written)—How produced by Mrs. Kane, 172, 196.

INDEX.

MESSAGES ("Spirit")—Internal evidence sufficient to prove their falsity, 162.

MERCENARY campaign—Begins in Rochester, 121, 126.—Tour of principal cities, 212, 222.

MOVEMENT of knees of "medium" noted by Dr. Lee while "raps" were heard, 143.

ORIGIN of the fraud, 81, 83, 87, 92.

PERSECUTION of Mrs. Catherine Fox Jencken and her children by spiritualistic enemies, 60.

PROPHECY of Dr. Kane concerning the future of Maggie Fox, 213.

PROMISES of Maggie Fox to Dr. Kane never to "rap" any more, 223, 226.

PRESIDENT Pierce's wife and Maggie Fox, 223.

PROFESSION of spiritualistic belief—Mrs. Kane expressly disclaims it, 181, 234.

"RAPS"—Failure to "throw" them to different parts of a room, 184.—Always heard near the spot where "medium" is stationed, 136, 172, 173.—Effort of the will in producing them apparent, 136.—Muscular contractions their possible cause, 137.—Not produced while "mediums" in constrained position, 142.—Not produced while feet of "mediums" are prevented from touching sonorous substances, 185.—Vibrations in foot of Mrs. Kane, felt by Mr. Sellers of the "Seybert Commission," 194.—Their physiological origin, 202, 203.

REPENTANCE—Mrs. Catherine Fox Jencken, 58, 59.—Mrs. Margaret Fox Kane, 233.

REPORTS on investigations of "rappings," 134, 141, 149, 173.

ROCHESTER—Outlandish doings told by Mrs. Underhill, 106, 113.—Mrs. Kane gives the true explanation of them, 112.—First public appearances of the Fox Sisters, 121.

SENATE ridicules Spiritualism in debate, 159.

SLADE (Henry) admits that certain magicians produce their effects in the same way that he does, 199.

SEYBERT (Henry)—Crazed by Spiritualism, 166.—Mrs. Kane

enters the "Spiritual Mansion," 164.—She draws the line at the Apostles and the Angel Gabriel, 166.—His legacy for the investigation of Spiritualism, 167.—His "spirit" mistakes the identity of a member of the "Seybert Commission" and calls him by a queer name, 171.—Though he knew no Latin in the flesh, his "spirit" is made to write Latin, 197.

"SEYBERT Commission" (The)—Its origin and labors, 167.—Experiments with Mrs. Kane, 169.—Its conclusions regarding the "rappings," 168, 201.—On other phases of Spiritualism, 201.

SPIRITUALISM—Mrs. Catherine Fox Jencken says it is the greatest curse the world has ever known, 56.

SUPERSTITION—Traditions in the Fox family about queer happenings, 119.

UNDERHILL (Ann Leah)—Her narrative proven false, 88.—Sinister influence over her younger sisters, 233.

VERDICT (The unalterable), 201.

VIBRATION of articles when "medium's" body is in contact with them while producing raps, 138, 145,

WARNINGS of Dr. Kane to Maggie and Katie Fox against a life of deception, 216, 219, 222, 225, 228, 229.—Against intercourse with her sister, Leah, 227.

FINIS.

www.ingramcontent.com/pod-product-compliance
Lightning Source LLC
Chambersburg PA
CBHW020801230426
43666CB00007B/800